Psychodrama, Surplus Reality and the Art of Healing

The practice of psychodrama allows participants to enter a realm of what might not be possible in life. This freedom from ordinary conventions is what Moreno called 'Surplus Reality', and is one of the most vital, curative and mysterious elements of psychodrama. However, even Moreno himself wrote very little about this essential part of the psychodramatic process.

In this book, Leif Dag Blomkvist and Zerka Moreno explore the depths of this long-neglected concept. With intelligence and humour, expressing the essence of the ideal psychotherapeutic mind and heart, Zerka Moreno explains the philosophy and practice of psychodrama, group psychotherapy and sociometry and their meaning for the human being in psychotherapy and the world at large. In addition, each chapter is prefaced by Leif Dag Blomkvist's explanations and illuminations of the forces and energies – from early religious rituals and festivals to the art of surrealism – which have influenced psychodrama.

In a book that is both intelligent and enriching, the authors show how surplus reality can change lives. Psychodramatists and mental health professionals who wish to take therapy beyond the 'verbal' will find the book valuable reading.

Zerka T. Moreno has practised psychodrama (of which she is co-creator) for almost 60 years. She has written numerous professional articles and is in demand all over the globe as a conference presenter and teacher.

Leif Dag Blomkvist is Director of the Swedish Moreno Institute and executive director of the Nordic Board of Examiners in Psychodrama, Sociometry and Group Psychotherapy.

Thomas Rützel works in private practice as a psychotherapist in Germany.

Psychodrama, Surplus Reality and the Art of Healing

Zerka T. Moreno,
Leif Dag Blomkvist and
Thomas Rützel

Routledge
Taylor & Francis Group
LONDON AND NEW YORK

First published 2000 by Routledge
2 Park Square, Milton Park, Abingdon, Oxfordshire OX14 4RN

Simultaneously published in the USA and Canada
by Taylor & Francis Inc
711 Third Avenue, New York, NY 10017

First issued in paperback 2014

Routledge is an imprint of the Taylor and Francis Group, an informa company

Typeset in Times by Keystroke, Jacaranda Lodge, Wolverhampton

British Library Cataloguing in Publication Data
A catalogue record for this book is available from the British Library

Library of Congress Cataloging in Publication Data
Moreno, Zerka T. (Zerka Toeman)
Psychodrama, surplus reality and the art of healing / Zerka T. Moreno, Leif Dag Blomkvist and Thomas Rützel.
p. cm.
Includes bibliographical references and index.
1. Psychodrama. I. Blomkvist, Leif Dag. II. Rützel, Thomas. III. Title.
RC489.P7 M65 2000
616.89'1523–dc21 99-045591

ISBN 978-0-415-22320-1 (hbk)
ISBN 978-0-415-75825-3 (pbk)

There is a knowing
and a not knowing.
There is a seeing
and a not seeing.
There is a hearing
and a not hearing.
There is a feeling
and a not feeling.
There is a being
and a not being.

All these
I've known
and seen
and heard
and felt
and been.
(Z. Moreno 1971)

Contents

Preface

Unfortunately, surplus reality is a dimension of psychodrama about which very little has been written. Even J.L. Moreno, originator of the method, did not publish much on this subject, although it might be considered one of the most vital, curative and mysterious elements of psychodrama.

For this book, three generations of psychodrama directors came together: Zerka Moreno, partner of J.L. in life and work; her student Leif Dag Blomkvist, trainer of psychodrama, developer, refiner, and teacher of surrealist psychodrama; and his student Thomas Rützel. The authors conceived this book simply because it covers ground not dealt with in the same manner or context in any previous literature about psychodrama. It is not only for therapists of whatever persuasion, but is equally valid for philosophers, dramatists, and other humanists.

Here, in her own words as told to Leif Dag Blomkvist, Zerka Moreno explains this long-neglected concept, which challenges orthodox ideas about psychotherapy, both group and individual. Although psychodrama is an action method, written words also carry a soul, which readers will experience as they read Mrs Moreno's spoken ones. She takes us with her back to the origins of J.L. Moreno's psychotherapeutic ideas and methods, and describes his revolutionary, humanistic alternative. With intelligence and humour, expressing the essence of the ideal psychotherapeutic mind and heart, Mrs Moreno explains the philosophy and practice of psychodrama, group psychotherapy and sociometry and their meaning for the human being in psychotherapy as well as the world at large.

Notes from Leif Dag Blomkvist

The original interviews with Zerka Moreno were made in 1992, 1993, 1995, and 1998 at Myrtle Beach, South Carolina. They covered a range of subjects, which then became chapters in this book. During the editorial process a chapter on clinical applications (three case studies) and an epilogue were included. I have added an introduction to each chapter (distinguishable by italics). Not part of the interviews, they were introduced to aid the reader in getting focused on the sometimes-complicated subject matter.

When I was a young student at the Moreno Institute in Beacon, New York, I sometimes had private conversations with Dr Moreno. My personal feelings toward him were ambiguous. On one hand I was struck by his *spiritus perversus*, i.e. his mind that turned things upside down, so that I never felt safe with him. On the other hand, he was a true creator. With Zerka Moreno I was able to establish a much closer relationship over the years.

On one of these occasions when Dr Moreno and I had a conversation, I understood how much he loved Zerka, not only as his wife and spiritual companion, but with the deepest respect for her as a trainer. He said to me, 'Many men have great ideas but they need someone who listens to them, understands them, transforms their ideas and spreads them into the world. You see, Dag, I had the idea but Zerka was my tool. Without her I could not have made it.'

In his book *Who Shall Survive?* Moreno writes: 'Creativity without spontaneity becomes lifeless, its living intensity increases and decreases in proportion to the amount of spontaneity in which it partakes. Spontaneity without creativity is empty and runs abortive' (Moreno 1953: 40). Spontaneity materializes creativity in interaction with people. So J.L. Moreno as the creative part and Zerka Moreno as the spontaneous part complemented each other in a unique way.

Readers of this book will also become aware of how much personal experience and suffering a person goes through to be able to experience the joy and full meaning of psychodrama. By reading Zerka Moreno in her own words, they will get to know a woman who used every struggle in her life concerning family, war, and disease, to broaden her wisdom in a truly humanitarian way.

Notes from Thomas Rützel, Interview editor

The first psychodrama seminar of my training was in 1985, directed by Leif Dag Blomkvist. Since then he has been my main psychodrama trainer, supervisor, and in the past few years colleague and loyal friend. After nine years I still admire him for his inspiration, wit, courage, honesty, and, not least of all, hard work. I also very much enjoy the privilege of being asked for advice and help in the editing of his articles and training programmes.

In 1993 I met Zerka Moreno for the first time at an international trainers' weekend in upstate New York. That is where the idea was conceived that my thesis for the title of Psychodrama Leader could be the editing of the interviews that Dag Blomkvist did with Zerka Moreno. I hope the readers of this book will enjoy this encounter with her as much as I did while editing.

Notes from Zerka Moreno

As for me, having experienced psychodrama for almost sixty years now, I have come to think of it as 'The Theatre of Mercy'. It is a place where love and acceptance of what we think of as the worst aspects of ourselves are found. We experience our common humanity and learn what it truly means to be human. We learn to transcend the past and reach for a more promising future.

There is a technique in psychodrama known as 'doubling'. A therapeutic actor stands or sits or walks next to the protagonist and assists that person to express him- or herself more fully. Perhaps the very best description of psychodrama I have ever encountered was given me by a client. 'I know what psychodrama is', she declared, 'it is the double of life.'

Acknowledgements

We would like to express our gratitude to Marc Treadwell for his comments and his contributions to the final manuscript.

Toni Horvatin provided invaluable editorial consultation and assistance, in some cases writing and reworking passages for continuity and clarity. She also produced and refined the manuscript and coordinated pre-production details.

Special thanks to Joanne Forshaw, editorial assistant at Routledge, for her pleasant, professional manner and patient assistance. We are also grateful to Imogen Burch, Senior Production Editor at Psychology Press Ltd, who was our expert guide in bringing this process to completion.

Finally, we would like to thank the countless protagonists, clients, students, and colleagues who have enabled and enriched our understanding of these concepts. Without them, this book could never have been written.

The authors would also like to thank the publishers Alfred A. Knopf, a division of Random House, Inc. for permission to quote from *The Prophet* by K. Gibran (1923).

An early history of psychodrama

Zerka T. Moreno

Considering that J.L. Moreno, the pioneer of psychodrama, sociometry, and a special approach to group psychotherapy, was educated at the University of Vienna Medical School where Sigmund Freud lectured and where both met in 1912, why did not Moreno become a psychoanalyst? After all, psychoanalysis was the very first school of personality investigation. At that time Freud was looking for spiritual sons, as some of his followers were turning psychoanalysis to other directions.

Why was Moreno not able to align himself with Freud? He reported in *Psychodrama: First Volume* that he went to hear Freud speak on Telepathic Dreams. At the end of the lecture, which Moreno noted with appreciation Freud delivered from bare notes, not from a written paper, Freud stood at the door as those present left the room, shook hands with each one, and asked them questions about themselves and in what they were engaged. At that time Moreno was a clinical assistant at the medical school and was allowed to wear the white coat, which he evidently wore to the lecture. When Moreno's turn came, so he stated, Freud noted his professional identity and asked him what his interest was and if he enjoyed the lecture, apparently treating Moreno as a junior colleague. The latter's retort is often quoted as a sample of his own philosophy of treatment:

> Well, Dr Freud, I start where you leave off. You meet people in the artificial setting of your office, I meet them on the street and in their home, in their natural surroundings. You analyze their dreams. I try to give them the courage to dream again. *I teach the people how to play God.*
>
> (J.L. Moreno 1977: 5–6)

In his answer to Freud, Moreno was not speaking of dream therapy. He alluded to the fact that helping people to dream their lives anew was his mode of assuring them that their lives could be improved if they harnessed their creativity and spontaneity. Even their most outrageous fantasy could be productive as long as it did not harm others. He noted that Freud appeared perplexed and made no response. Probably such ideas he considered megalomaniacal and therefore rather dangerous. But that was only part of Moreno's view of the life of the mind and of the basic difference between Freud and himself.

One of the ways in which Moreno elucidated the differences between Freud and himself was to remind us that Freud dealt only with the individual psyche, referring the psychic energy to libido which, according to him, is constant from birth. For Moreno that energy is not only an individual source but related to the group and the cosmos, fuelled by spontaneity/creativity.

'We are more than economic, psychological, biological or sociological beings, we are first and foremost cosmic beings. We come from the cosmos and we return there', he often declared. He did not spell it out in any detail but he had written a book called *The Words of the Father* (German original *Das Testament das Vaters*), in which he proclaimed that God's voice is in all of us, he just happened to hear that voice directly inside him and wrote down what he heard. In psychiatric terms that transcendental experience might have been diagnosed as paranoia.

Clearly, the divide between Moreno and Freud was unbridgeable at that time. Nevertheless, whatever the differences between them, they were both charismatic and unique personalities. That quality made them both extraordinary psychotherapists.

There is a rather amusing addendum to this story. When Moreno was still a student at the university, he decided one fine day to grow a beard. Oddly, that was not considered proper for young men at the time and reminds us of the 60s when many of the younger generation of males started to grow them as a way of demonstrating both their manhood and independence from the older generation. It is conceivable that both these ideas stimulated Moreno. At the time, only the professors wore beards and when Moreno was accosted about his and asked why he was growing it, his response was: 'It just grows naturally', as if to indicate that it was not his intention to interfere with nature. Picture, therefore, the above confrontation of an old beard with a young one: Freud's as neatly trimmed as a formal English garden, Moreno's growing as it would, untouched by trimmers, shears, scissors, or razor blades. Somehow the symbolism is rather potent in its silence. Freud was looking for sons, being the father of his ideas; Moreno stating without words that he was not about to be anyone's son but was himself a father of ideas and in search of sons.

There were, however, still other reasons why Moreno did not believe in psychoanalysis. He did not assume that words alone were able to convey the entire psyche. He did not believe mere speech is the royal route into that psyche, but sensed that there is a more primordial level which underlies speech, namely the level of the act and interact. Observing children's behaviour he came to the idea that the human being has a hunger for action – physical action as well as action of the mind. Moreno was aware that these same children learned an enormous amount long before they spoke, living and absorbing their environment intensely. So he taught that phylogenetically and ontogenetically, from the point of view of the human race and that of the individual, speech is a fairly late development in the human being. However, the child is in interaction with others from the moment of birth and absorbs all kinds of learning, good, bad and indifferent, but learning. The child asks itself: 'Is the universe friendly?' Regrettably, for far too many, it is not. Nevertheless, if left somewhat to its own devices, there is a positive 'Yes' from the child, a 'Yes' to life. This capacity to engage joyously with life Moreno assessed to be due to spontaneity and creativity, which he considered to be *the central problem* of humanity: how to continue to face life with all that it entails with a capacity, not merely to adapt, but to surmount the barriers and obstacles it presents. He noted that this kind of freedom diminishes in many of us and needs a special environment in which to blossom.

Moreno has described how, at age 4 or 5, he played God while sitting on a high chair, as on a throne, which his playmates had constructed on top of a table in the basement of his home in Bucharest. He had organized a game with them, playing God and His Angels, and he, of course, must be God. When one of the angels started 'flying', she asked him why he was not flying. Never one to shirk a challenge, he did, fell onto the floor and broke his right arm.

Years later, telling this story Moreno added: 'Since then I consider that psychodrama is the therapy for fallen gods'. To him, every human being was a genius but some lived that better than others. He chose to reinstate them if he could. It was also one reason he was so fond of children, who are both closer to their genius and to God, and of psychotic patients who have lost their way. It was only gradually that psychodrama began to be appreciated as a way of personal growth for those of us who are no longer children, nor altogether psychotic, but who can still find a better path.

Moreno was inspired by the great religions of our world. He admired Socrates as a teacher but stated that Jesus was a greater healer than anyone, himself or his contemporaries. He pointed out that Jesus did not wait in a little room somewhere away from his community for people to come to him for help, that he went out into that world with all its dangers, found the sufferers and healed them then and there.

As a student of philosophy Moreno wandered in the many gardens of Vienna and began to engage children by telling them all kinds of fantastic stories. As he found them listening, he decided to enact both his and their stories as well as fairy tales which were part of their culture. Much of his later theory on child development was based on these experiences. He noted the children's passion to jump up and embody the characters brought forth verbally and decided that the human being is an improvising actor on the stage of life.

To return to the problem Moreno saw with using language alone as a therapeutic tool, he pointed out that one's philosophy of therapy influences how the client's words would be interpreted. Thus there is no universally suitable interpretation, and worse, there is no universal language. Besides, if language were the all important tool for communication, why do we have music, dance, mime, sculpture, painting, etc.? Are these not tools for communication? But of what a different sort!

Moreno searched for a new and different model, one that would be more lifelike and complete in its ability to reach and communicate the deeper layers of the mind, as well as offering greater flexibility than did life itself. He began to explore the drama as a possible avenue. As a student of philosophy he had studied Greek and Latin and it was the most advanced form of drama known in the Western world to which he turned his attention, that of the Greeks.

In Aristotle's *Poetics* he found what that philosopher described as 'catharsis' or purging of two emotions when spectators are watching a tragedy, namely pity for the tragic hero or heroine, and fear – in some translations it appears as terror or awe – for oneself, should anything similar ever happen in one's own life. Aristotle's idea was that this effect upon spectators would be beneficial, that they would leave the theatre in a purified, cleansed mood. Moreno declared that this was at best an 'esthetic catharsis', not a purely emotional one. After all, the spectators were aware that these were actors portraying the characters, not themselves, however splendid the poet's ability to bring them to life. Thus, he reasoned, it was a secondary catharsis, not a primary one. He wondered how the roles affected the actors and whether they obtained a catharsis from playing them. When he later began to work with actors he found that indeed a great number suffered from a histrionic neurosis because many fragments of various roles stuck to their insides and remained unintegrated, often disturbing them and also invading and unbalancing their private lives.

So he questioned further: What would happen if the roles were taken away altogether in this finished form, if the script was thrown away, and the actors were allowed to perform their own concerns and troubles? Would there be new forms of catharsis enabled, for instance, the catharsis of the actor as well as a primary catharsis of the spectator? The latter would know that these are real tears, real laughter, genuinely personal emotions that were being expressed and enacted, not merely rehearsed and recreated ones.

Once Moreno's medical studies were behind him, this idea of improvising roles became a more defined preoccupation which led to his organizing a Theatre of Spontaneity, in which improvisation became an art form, giving the actors opportunities to be creative and spontaneously shape their roles. He wanted to prove that this was a legitimate form of theatre, more so than the so-called legitimate theatre where everything is rehearsed and repeated, finished and polished, but, as he termed it, a 'cultural conserve', a frozen product which stifled spontaneity and creativity of the actors, much the way children's spontaneity is stifled by our culture, especially when they start going to regular school.

The definition coined by J.L. Moreno of spontaneity was: a new response to an old situation, and also: an adequate response to a new situation. It is when our roles become stereotyped that we are in trouble, then they need to be infused with creativity and spontaneity, renewed and refreshed and even changed. By 'adequate' he did not mean a standard response, he meant integrative for all concerned even if that meant sometimes upsetting the partner in the interactive role at first, eventually leading to new and important learning.

The Theatre of Spontaneity was part of a revolution in drama, namely the art of improvisation. That revolution had already begun in the early years of the century, especially in Russia. There is no doubt that it was part of the *Zeitgeist*. But no one before him had carried out such a consistent effort of creating a theatre specifically for the purpose of proving that spontaneity and creativity are special functions of the human mind. Unfortunately, these qualities were not respected in the way that intelligence, memory, motor control and particularly conformity of behaviour are in the Western cultures. They needed to be acknowledged, respected and appreciated. He was not only concerned with improving theatre, he wanted our everyday lives to be improved, to be filled with these spontaneous–creative urges which somehow, especially in childhood, get squelched and distorted, and, in many cases, disfigured.

It was almost by accident that this improvisational theatre turned one evening into a theatre of therapy. One of Moreno's female actors developed what he designated a 'histrionic neurosis'. He coined that term in the 20s. Today it has even become a psychiatric category.

The actor in question, whom Moreno called Barbara, had been typecast as a model of pure womanhood. In fact, she was a regular at portraying the Virgin Mary at the passion plays at Easter. She had recently married a poet, named George by Moreno, who came to watch her nightly in the Theatre of Spontaneity. One evening he sought out Moreno before the performance to tell him of his woes. He spoke of how that selfsame, lovely, virginal creature, so much adored and admired by all, was the perfect opposite at home, a living hellion in fact. He claimed that she used abusive street language such as he had never heard and which was certainly unacceptable in their stratum. He was beginning to find her behaviour unbearable and asked Moreno if he could somehow intervene.

It just happened that Moreno had instituted a form within the Theatre of Spontaneity that he called 'The Living Newspaper' (*Die Lebendige Zeitung*). The main reason for developing this aspect of the performances was to prove the spontaneity and creativity of the actors. If they portrayed the news of that day on the spot, they could not be accused of having had time to rehearse it. He had found this manoeuvre necessary because a number of drama critics who came to evaluate the new experiment declared, when the enactment went smoothly, that it must have been rehearsed, but when it did not, they contended that improvisational theatre did not work. It was not a win–win situation.

To gather the news of the day, Moreno turned his actors into reporters and sent them out into the streets to pick up newsworthy items. On the aforementioned evening, one of the actors, on his quest for material for The Living Newspaper, had brought in a choice item of news, namely that a prostitute had been murdered by her pimp in an argument over money which he accused her of holding out on him. This was just the initiative Moreno needed to address Barbara, the actor, and to suggest to her that her repertoire was becoming stale, too restricted, that she needed to play other roles, roles of women of the lower depths, that it was time for her to explore such roles. She agreed that she, too, had felt stale and was ready to try it. 'But', she asked him: 'do you think I can do it?' 'I have every confidence in you', he declared knowingly.

According to Moreno, she was a great hit that evening and gradually she became a more versatile actor. By the way, the male actor portraying the pimp was none other than Peter Lorre, a young man Moreno had discovered. He later made a film in Germany, *M*, in which he played a child murderer. Still later he went to Hollywood and openly declared his training with Moreno in Vienna to be the only acting lessons he ever had.

The poet/husband came to report to Moreno that Barbara's behaviour slowly improved: from time to time she laughed when she fell into her former habit, remembering she had done that in the theatre. Being able to laugh at oneself and one's failings is surely already a step towards healing since it involves developing distance from some part of the self.

From a technical viewpoint, it is important to note what Moreno was after. Having observed the stifling and distorting of Barbara's creativity and spontaneity due to the roles she played having become conserves in themselves, this opportunity to break out of that pattern and give her a fresh ability made a great deal of sense. It later became part of the retraining process for persons whose life roles were equally becoming frozen.

Moreno asked Barbara and George to spontaneously enact together some of the scenes from their marriage. These became a regular feature of the theatre's performances. Parenthetically, this was a pioneering effort in couples and marital therapy through what later became psychodrama. When members of the audience declared to him that these scenes touched them more deeply than the others, the idea arose in him that this might be the beginning of a new form of theatre altogether – a theatre for healing, not only for the actors, but for the persons watching it.

This was the fruit of Moreno's original deep intellectual questioning of the nature of catharsis. It made complete sense out of the performance of Barbara and her husband and the intense response of the spectators to these enactments.

It would not be correct to report that henceforth this form of theatre became Moreno's major preoccupation since he had other creative ideas on which he was working; but the seedlings for further development were in the background for many years to come.

The Theatre of Spontaneity ran in Vienna from about 1922 to 1925, when Moreno migrated to the United States and took his ideas, hoping to have them take root and flourish there. He would say that 'Psychodrama was conceived in Vienna but born in America'.

The idea that we are improvising actors on life's very own stage is a powerful one. It is obvious that many of us do not do it very well and require help. The notion that there is another form of drama, one that will respect us even when we fail and teach us how to live more fully and creatively, eventually developed into psychodrama, the drama of the mind. It is a form of drama which releases realms of our being that were always there in our infancy but which had no proper channels for fulfilment. Moreno sometimes described it as 'a laboratory for learning how to live.' Remember that no one acts alone, we are co-actors here on earth and it is especially there where we have tremendous difficulties and obstacles to overcome. How we do it determines whether we are in disharmony or in concert with others.

Introduction

Everyone who has ever participated in a psychodrama is both fascinated and stunned by the impact of spontaneous play. This form of theatre starts on an empty stage with no script, no professional actors and no rehearsals. There is only the protagonist with his or her story which through the unique psychodramatic techniques expands into a full play, be it tragedy, satire or comedy. The psychodrama has a strong psychological impact on the protagonist, the co-actors and the group present. There is no audience in psychodrama. The persons present are all part of the play. Everything takes place on the stage in full view, in the here and now, and can never be reproduced. Psychodrama is not merely a theatre of expression, as many believe, because it is also a theatre of restraint. It is, according to us, only tangentially linked to expressive therapies. Psychodrama is better defined as the Theatre of Encounter, in fact, it *is* encounter and confrontation, an *Auseinandersetzung* (German, meaning, 'to be set apart').

It is the Theatre of Ecstasy in its purest sense as well as in the literal sense of the word because it forces the individual to step outside his or her limited world and dissolves borders. In psychodrama men can play women and vice versa, the young can play the old and vice versa, one can play an aeroplane or any kind of object, a body part, an idea, or even God. Everything is brought into an encounter with someone or something else, or with parts of the self, all of which relate. This world without limits, where the person is liberated from the real world, is what Moreno called 'surplus reality', and this is what this book is about.

Unfortunately Moreno wrote very little on this subject. In an article for *Group Psychotherapy* he wrote:

> Psychodrama consists not merely of the enactment of episodes, past, present and future, which are experienced and conceivable within the framework of reality – a frequent misunderstanding. There is in

> psychodrama a mode of experience, which goes beyond reality, which provides the subject with a new and more extensive experience of reality, a *surplus reality*. I was influenced to coin the term 'surplus reality' by Marx's concept of 'surplus value'. Surplus value is part of the earnings of the worker of which he is robbed by capitalistic employers. But surplus reality is, in contrast, not a loss but an enrichment of reality by the investments and extensive use of imagination. This expansion of experience is made possible in psychodrama by methods not used in life – auxiliary egos, auxiliary chair, double, role reversal, mirror, magic shop, the high chair, the psychodramatic baby, soliloquy, rehearsal of life, and others.
>
> (J.L. Moreno 1965, 4: 212–213)

Because this is one of the few sources on this subject his successors took it upon themselves to explore and explain the concept of surplus reality. Surplus reality is a vital healing instrument for the group as well as for the individual because sessions take place in this almost mystical and alchemical realm. Alchemy is the science of transmutation. According to Freud, psychotherapy as an idea was always better understood by humanists, artists, archaeologists, philosophers and writers than by practitioners of medical science. Psychodrama is both a science and an art. The artistry resides in the skills of the director.

Moreno stated that the aim of the Viennese *Stegreiftheater* ('Theatre of Spontaneity') was to bring about a revolution of the theatre.

> It attempted this change in a fourfold manner:
>
> 1 The elimination of the playwright and of the written play.
> 2 Participation of the audience, a 'theatre without spectators'. Everyone is a participant, everyone is an actor.
> 3 The actors and the audience are now the only creators. Everything is improvised, the play, the action, the motive, the words, the encounter and the resolution of the conflicts.
> 4 The old stage has disappeared, in its place steps the open stage, the space stage, the open space, the space of life, life itself.
>
> (J.L. Moreno 1973: a)

These ideas of breaking with traditional rules had already been presented by many other creators. The idea of impromptu theatre was also explored in 1916 by the Zurich Dada Movement's Cabaret Voltaire. The Dada movement has actually very little to do with Moreno's sociometric revolution but the Cabaret Voltaire was famous for its impulsive, spontaneous creations. The Dadaist experienced the world as *rational madness*. According to this view, art and literature disguised and mystified reality, science was exploited for military purposes, and philosophy was used to turn human thinking into slavery. Dada became a catalyst for the revolutionary moods; it was cultural paroxysm. It wanted to create a *tabula rasa* of the entire world. Philosophically Tristan Tzara and Moreno had one thing in common: both asserted the importance of change and surprise. They were both against psychoanalysis. Tzara believed that psychoanalysis puts man's irrational fantasies to sleep by analysing them. Moreno wrote of the climate during his time at the University of Vienna (where he met Freud):

> psychoanalysis had developed an atmosphere of fear among young people. Fear of neurosis was the measure of the day. A heroic gesture, a noble aspiration made its bearer immediately suspect. . . . After purging nature (Darwin) and society (Marx) from creative cosmic forces, the final step was the purging of genius by psychoanalysis. It was the revenge of the mediocre mind to bring everything down to its lowest common denominator. . . . All men are geniuses. . . . An army of Philistines fall over Samson. He was admired and feared for no reason. He is not stronger than we are. . . . Everyone can let his hair grow.
>
> (J.L. Moreno 1977: 6)

Moreno and the Dada movement opened the doors to a world unknown. The Dada movement dissolved itself and merged into the surrealistic movement led by André Breton. The surrealist movement became one of the most vital currents of modern poetry, art and revolutionary thought.

Surplus reality and surrealism are as related to one another as they are separate. When one thinks of the world-renowned productions of surrealist painters such as Magritte, Dali, Miro, they all praised this dimension of existence, which goes beyond reality. Breton defined surrealism in this way:

> Surrealism, *n. masc.* pure psychic automatism, by which an attempt is made to express, either verbally, in writing or in any other manner, the true functioning of thought. The dictation of thought, in the absence of all control by the reason, excluding any aesthetic or moral preoccupation.
>
> (Breton 1965: 89)

That statement is in opposition to Morenian thought and the Morenian concept of spontaneity, because spontaneity involves reflection, conscious control and moral as well as ethical considerations. It involves including the other. The surrealists also became more interested in Freud and in his concept of the unconscious, and their automatism has much in common with Freud's method of free association. Freud as well as the surrealists must have drawn the same conclusion, i.e., that the unconscious and the entire psychological world is inside the body. Moreno questioned this narrow view. Who says that the psyche is inside the body? Has anyone ever 'seen' a psyche? Moreno postulated in 1943 in an article 'Sociometry and the Cultural Order,' that:

> The biological picture of an individual places the psyche within the body (as an epi-phenomenon). In the sociometric picture of the individual (person) the psyche appears as outside the body, the body is surrounded by the psyche and the psyche is surrounded by and interwoven into the social and cultural atoms.
>
> (J.L. Moreno 1943: 319)

Moreno believed psyche and *materia* are not necessarily separated. Therefore, he regarded the distinction between conscious and unconscious as superficial and not functional on the psychodrama stage since surplus reality dissolves that distinction.

The surrealists embraced the world of dreams, of reaching the psyche by drugs, by creating exhaustion as well as other means to encounter this archaic world. Many surrealist painters, in fact, became insane and committed suicide. As the Swiss Jungian psychoanalyst Marie-Luise von Franz stated, the encounter with the unconscious is not a picnic on the lawn and has to be done with care and concern. Psychodrama is what Moreno called 'controlled acting out'. The individual is not by him-/herself, the experience is shared by the group present.

However, psychodrama encompasses also a great deal of what might be called 'surrealistic experience'. When one steps upon the psychodrama stage the subsequent production rarely turns out to be like the images one had during the warm-up. While on the stage, enacting one's images, the psychodrama finds its own course, takes over and brings its own direction. The purpose of the director is to assist that process as spontaneously as possible. This moment between one's ideas and one's action we may refer to as 'the surreal experience', a moment of not knowing; here enters the concept of mastering these surprises with spontaneity, on the part of the actor, the co-actors and the director.

André Breton describes the surreal experience as:

> *De l'instant où pour les premiers navigateurs une nouvelle terre fut en vue à celui où ils mirent le pied sur la côte, de l'instant où tel savant put se convaincre qu'il venait d'être témoin d'un phénomène jusqu'à lui inconnu à celui où il commença à mesurer la portée de son observation.*[1]
>
> (Breton 1937: 34)

The dream introduces a strange world that cannot be controlled, or only to a very small extent. One way to grasp the incomprehensible is to analyse the dream. Psychodrama will also introduce you to a world of estrangement, but it is not simply a dream and you are having this experience together with others, within a group. You influence the production and the dramatic quality. That is the profound difference between the surreal world and the world of surplus reality. It is a world which may never have been nor may ever be, yet it is absolutely real. It is pignorative, that is, with power of redemption.

Chapter 1

Time and death

Time only exists in relation to an event that is happening here and now, that has happened in the past or will take place in the future. A moment must pass to become a moment, because the Now is timeless. When I say, 'Here I am', this statement is already past and therefore means, 'There I was'.

In many religions time was experienced as a godhead or its manifestation through a stream of life welling out of it. This stream of life can also be seen as the creative energy of the world. One can find this idea of a godhead being time or not-time itself in most of the ancient religions.

The ancient Greeks, for example, regarded their god of time, Aion, as a vital fluid in living beings, a fluid that continued its existence even after death in the form of a snake. That reminds one of the Ouroborus, the snake that bites its tail. Time was seen as the basic substance of the universe from which fire, air and water arose. Marie-Luise von Franz writes:

> *Aion, the god of time, is here clearly an image of the dynamic aspect of existence, of what we might call today a principle of psycho-physical energy. All opposites – change and duration, even good and evil, life and death – are included in this cosmic principle.*
>
> *(von Franz 1992: 65)*

However, in the Judaeo-Christian tradition God is understood as being outside of time. God created time when s/he created the world. With the creation of the sun and the moon and, consequently, the establishment of day and night, time came into existence. St Augustine, who thought much about time, said, 'If nobody asks me what time is, I know what it is, but when I have to explain it to someone I do not know.' The gap between the divine being, God, and the relative insignificance of the creature manifests itself, according to St Augustine, particularly in the relation between God's eternity and the mere temporality of everything created (Augustinus 1955).

How is it that time plays such an important role in our lives? How did it start? In ancient times priests wanted to determine certain days in the course of the year for certain rituals to be held. People achieved this, for example, by stone circles with which they could exactly measure the position of the sun as it constantly changes during the year's course. Later, smaller sundials were developed for measuring the time of day. The Greeks measured time with a so-called klepshydra *('water-stealer'). This was a container with a hole near the bottom and marks on its inside. On these marks the level of the water showed the elapsed time. A similar design was that of the sandglass or hourglass. Time was also measured by marks on candles burning down or by the decreasing level of oil in oil lamps. The real change came in the 14th century with the invention of the clock with a mechanical escapement, which was first built in church towers. With these aids time in the form of hours which were now equal in length and objectively measurable permeated into man's psyche. Thus man's perception and consciousness of time became of lasting influence.*

DAG: Zerka, could you tell me something about the concept of time in psychodrama and its relationship to death?

ZERKA: When we are young, we have a very long future and only a short past. As we go through life, that balance changes. In mid-life, we have a longer past and a shorter future; and, as we age, we have an even longer past and an even shorter future. During this process the experience of time takes on different dimensions. Time seems endless when you are young. But as you age you experience it as going faster and faster.

An example could be a story from my family. My mother's grandmother, after whom I am named, was the only one in our family who lived to be 90 years old. When they celebrated her 80th birthday my mother was 18. So here you see youth and advancing age. My mother asked: 'Grandmother – 80 years, is that a very long time?' because for her it seemed an eternity. And her grandmother answered her: 'My child, do you see this room? It's like coming in through the door, going through the room, and going out the other end.'

Chronology plays a very important role for human beings in the experience of time. Time is actually a man-made construct and man invented the clock to measure it. Man is the measure and the measurer of all things. Even the ancients measured time in terms of the sun's daily movement and the moon's waning and waxing within the month (a word that derives from the word 'moon'). But they did not invent the mechanical clock, which is independent from sun or moon cycles, and a great invention.

Animals do not know about time. Their rhythm of life is linked to the sun's rhythm as it changes throughout the seasons. That is another dimension in the experience of time which may also have been the experience of our prehistoric ancestors.

DAG: In the story about your great-grandmother you mentioned that the course of life is like passing through a room. Where do you go to out the other end?

ZERKA: You reach a third dimension in the experience of time, that of eternity or the timeless. Eternity is related to the Cosmos[1] from whence we came and to which we return, and that is a mystery.

DAG: How important has this concept of man being of cosmic origin been in your directing?

ZERKA: The cosmic experience is a spiritual experience, an experience of 'there is no time; there is no time limit'.

My way of directing in this sense is: I have to forget about human time and open up or even take away the frontiers. In psychodrama you can weave from past to present to future and back again.

That, of course, leads to surplus reality, a significant concept in psychodrama. It is beyond man's measure of time. The future is an example of surplus reality and it is also beyond time. Or imagine you look at a picture showing a mountain. What would you say the space in distance is between you and the mountain? This point of view is very fascinating because for me it refers to the philosophical problem of space and time. The distance is immeasurable and, therefore, cosmic.

There is also the problem: To which distance does the question refer? Is it the distance between me and the picture I hold in my hands, or is it the distance I would have to cover to get to this mountain? And regarding the dimension of time I could ask myself: Is this a picture of a mountain which may even not exist any longer? There is still the picture, but the mountain may have ceased to exist a long time ago.

DAG: Is there a relation between the concept of man-made time and the concept of the cultural conserve?

ZERKA: Time is a conserve. It is a frozen thing. However, in a way it is an end product, just as books are an end product. No man has made time in that sense. God, or whatever you want to name that creative power, made the world and thus time. We divided it up into blocks of time.

To mark an event we have to give an exact time, date, and place. Seen this way time is a frozen moment. In contrast to this the Greek philosopher Heraclitus is reported to have said: 'Everything flows, nothing subsists.' And thus time flows. The stages of our life could be compared to a river which is, at the same time, in all places: the well, the rapids, the waterfall, and the mouth of the river. There is only presence, not a shadow of future. We could look upon our life accordingly. We are connected to our childhood, to our mature age, and to our old age. There are no frontiers. It is only we who cut time into little pieces such as minutes, seconds, milliseconds, and so forth.

DAG: What is the Morenian definition of the cultural conserve ?

ZERKA: The cultural conserve as Moreno saw it is the end product of spontaneity and creativity. It is really taking a moment and freezing it in time. And to unfreeze that moment, you go back to the source, which is spontaneity and creativity. So it is both, the end product and the beginning of something new, swinging back and forth like a pendulum.

DAG: 'Cultural conserve' is often used by psychodramatists with a negative connotation because it is seen only as something frozen. But you also include the beginning.

ZERKA: Moreno thought it was negative if it prevented *new* spontaneity and creativity. If it *encouraged* new spontaneity and creativity, then it became like a well that does not dry up. However, if it prevents spontaneity and creativity, then it is negative and you become blocked. The spontaneity factor makes it possible to experience cultural conserves differently. Moreno gave the following example: you leave your house every morning at the same time to go to your job and, as every morning, you meet the postman. Can you muster enough spontaneity to experience this as a new moment every day? It's very difficult. In Germany you say: *Der mensch ist ein gewohnheitstier* ('Man is a creature of habit'). *Gewohnheit* or 'habit' means 'a frozen moment'. Can you encounter the postman with words like: 'Oh, good morning' and 'How are you this morning? Are you all right? How do you feel today?' as if this had never taken place before? Moreno felt that most of us do not have an enormous, special kind of creativity, like Beethoven or Rembrandt. What is important for us is to have this daily infusion of spontaneity and creativity in order to make life fresh and liveable. Spontaneity and creativity: experiencing newness, novelty, freshness, something in addition to, rather than something the same as what was before.

It was Meister Eckhart, the medieval mystic, who said that the most important moment in your life is the present, the most important person in your life is the one you talk to just now, the most important deed in your life is love. The eternal Now (Eckhart 1963).

Chapter 2

The moment of surprise

Moments of surprise are more common in our daily lives than we may think. There are surprises that are totally unexpected external events that impact us. There is another form of surprise which is more intrapsychic. For instance, one is surprised about the distance between one's expectation and actuality. In this moment of surprise the perception of reality is blown to pieces. The person suddenly finds him-/herself in a zone of transition where reality gets mixed up with hopes, fears and dreams. Both Moreno and the surrealist philosopher Breton gave this moment of transition much attention.

The Greeks honoured the god Dionysus as the god of surprise and transition. Walter Otto expresses this as follows:

> *The world man knows, the world in which he has settled himself so securely and snugly, that world is no more. The turbulence which accompanied the arrival of Dionysus has swept it away. Everything has been transformed. But it has not been transformed into a charming fairy tale or into an ingenuous child's paradise. The primeval world has stepped into the foreground, the depths of reality have been opened, the elemental forms of everything that is creative, everything that is destructive, have arisen, bringing with them infinite rapture and infinite terror. The innocent picture of a well-ordered routine world has been shattered by their coming, and they bring with them no illusions or fantasies but truth – a truth that brings on madness.*
>
> *(Otto 1981: 95)*

In surrealistic philosophy this moment of transition where people lose their ground and relate to images, fears and dreams also confronts them with an encounter with the unknown. Surrealists honoured this moment and regarded it as something very creative. André Breton writes:

> *C'est dans la surprise crée par une nouvelle image ou par une nouvelle association d'images, qu'il faut voir le plus important élément du progrès des sciences physiques, puisque c'est l'étonnement qui excite la logique, toujours assez froide, et qui l'oblige a établir de nouvelles coordinations.*[1]
>
> *(Breton 1949)*

Moreno thought that human beings are rather ill-prepared and ill-equipped to face the moments of surprise, which may be so because spontaneity is far less respected than memory and intelligence.

It seems that all three, the Mythologist, the surrealist and the Morenian consider the moment of surprise as a moment of transition in which one needs the role of the Creator.

DAG: Moreno implied that we do not take surprises very well. When we are children, surprises are something encouraging, challenging and delightful. But when we get older that attitude changes or vanishes and a rather fearful attitude towards surprises takes place. One may say that the ego then is more likely to cling to the well-known. What do surprises mean for people?

ZERKA: There are two opposing ways of encountering surprises: one is anxiety, and the other joy. There are surprises that challenge people in such a way that they are not sure how to handle them and they become insecure. That is where spontaneity must come in. Flowing with their spontaneity and creativity can fill that moment and reduce the anxiety. Remember that spontaneity and anxiety are functions of one another: when spontaneity increases, anxiety goes down, and vice versa. That is the first aspect. The other is joy.

The word 'spontaneity' comes from the Latin *sua sponte* which means from within the self, of one's own accord. It should not be understood as impulsive behaviour; rather the opposite. Spontaneity involves tele[2] and reflection and it also gives the person a feeling that s/he is free to act according to the situation. S/he is not encountering the situation with anxiety but with the feeling of being capable of mastering it.

The moment of surprise can lead to a transition from one state to another. However, very often the first response is shock. And if you do not master spontaneity to overcome the shock, you are stuck. So the first response usually is: 'My God, how did this happen; what do I do now?' Then spontaneity can arise, transition can take place. One door closes, another one opens. But, you will find that many people get stuck behind the closed door. We treat, for example, people with divorce problems. Those involved are often fixated in a long frozen moment. In psychodrama we bring them back to develop their own spontaneity. Thus they are enabled to master the situation. But there is also a chance for transition if spontaneity is equal to the challenge.

DAG: When patients are faced with such surprises as sudden death in the family, loss of their job, divorce, etc., many psychodrama directors tend to look for an explanation as a healing agent.

You pointed out the importance of warming up the protagonist to new spontaneity in order to deal with the situation. Would you please deepen that thought a little?

ZERKA: The basic difference between Moreno and Freud can be expressed this way: Freud would ask: 'What happened to you? Tell me, and I will interpret it for you.' Moreno would ask: 'How did you get here? And what does this situation consist of?', which he means sociometrically. 'And how can we get you out of it?' *What?* is a diagnostic question. *How?* is an action question. That's the difference. You do need to know *what*, but that's not what leads you out of it. It is the *how* that promotes the action out of the situation. I think that there is often confusion about this. 'How did I contribute to this?' People like to be in control. During that moment of surprise or shock we are out of control. So we want to establish a rationale[3] because that gives us a certain operative framework. 'This is what I have to do', or 'This is how I have to deal with it'.

I believe that is only a solution if one's behaviour truly changes. Moreno and I found that in psychotherapy knowing or having insight by itself does not cure. All it does is it gives you insight. To translate from insight into changed behaviour means, again, linking into spontaneity and creativity. What we as psychodramatists are concerned with is how you make the leap from insight into new action. That's the hard thing. Many people have lots of insight and know all about themselves. And then they come to you and say, 'I've been through this or that kind of therapy. Why can't I change?' That requires spontaneity and creativity.

What we're concerned with is not what you know about yourself, but what you *do* about yourself.

Chapter 3

Ecstasy and role reversal

Zerka regards psychodramatists to be practitioners of a craft who 'repair' human relations. Moreno created the psychodramatic stage on which people could train their capabilities to involve themselves in new and spontaneous encounters. Psychodrama's main intent is to establish or re-establish tele between people or between the different inner roles and figures.

One of the most important techniques to serve this purpose is role reversal. Role reversal means to look upon oneself through another person's eyes or from another person's perspective. To really see oneself from the perspective of another person one has to be warmed up to the role of the other for a substantial amount of time. This important aspect of time is often underestimated.

The technique of role reversal is an ecstatic and, therefore, a Dionysian tool on the psychodrama stage. Dionysus is the god of drama, theatre, and involvement. Role reversal is the technique of absolute involvement, to be able to see the plot from another point of view, whatever that may be. So the protagonist must really step outside the self and become the other person.

As a psychodrama director it is often amazing to see with how much pleasure protagonists take on the role of, for instance, somebody they really detest or someone who gives them a lot of trouble. They act out such roles with much mischievous and evil pleasure. They step outside themselves and enact sides of themselves they would never allow to be shown otherwise. They often show great pleasure in dressing up as this person and turning the enactment into a caricature.

In Greek drama, both tragedy and comedy, the actors were all substantially dressed up and masked.

> *A complete disguise was the external sign that the actor had given up

> *his own identity in honour of the god, in order to let another being speak and act through him. Dionysus, for whom the dramas were performed, was the god of ecstasy. The word ekstasis means 'standing outside oneself', in other words the renunciation of individuality.*
> *(Simon 1982: 10)*

DAG: Being trained by you I realized that you no longer work with a lot of auxiliary egos on the stage. Instead you keep the protagonist for considerable periods in the role of the other. After a while s/he usually starts to feel like this person and begins to look upon him-/herself with the eyes of the other. I regard this long warm-up of the protagonist in the role of the other as a true 'Zerka'-technique.

I once experienced it myself in a psychodrama you directed, in which you let me experience the life of my mother. The psychodrama dealt with my conviction that, when I was a boy, my mother gave me away out of selfishness so she could enjoy life more. After the session I felt differently about that situation and could start to relate more spontaneously to my mother. Today we have a rather good relationship.

ZERKA: The crucial word here is *perception*. When you enter a scene with your own perception, that is all you have. When you *truly* role-reverse there is a *shift of perception* either during or after the process. That's what changes and that's what role reversal is supposed to do, not give you knowledge or insight. Those are artefacts that come with the task. The essential learning is: 'Hey, from this perspective it's different from the way I saw it.' And then you can change your own perception in terms of this new learning.

DAG: Would you, therefore, say that directors should not so much focus on helping the protagonist to solve problems, but help him/her do the role reversal properly and let the process take care of itself afterwards?

ZERKA: Role reversal may be only the beginning. You may still have to guide that person into other scenes. Moreno taught us that all forms of psychotherapy should *tap the autonomous healing centre of the protagonist*. When psychodrama does not achieve this purpose, it is bad or incomplete psychodrama.

Clients or protagonists are persons who are free to act. They come to us with their problems, pain, and concerns. One way to change that is through their relationship to significant others. We are *relationship therapists*. You mentioned the psychodrama about your relationship to your mother where you honestly enacted parts of her life. Nobody can *totally* take the part of another human being. At best one can only approximate certain feelings. From this perspective no one has total perception of another human being. The perception may be lacking or weak, incomplete and often somewhat distorted, because that is part of being human. Perhaps there is a God or a creative power able to have such total perception. However, it is not given to mere mortals. But perception in the role of the other brings one very close to the essence of that other and sometimes includes feelings in the body and changes in size.

There were two men who came to training with us, two psychologists who had known each other since college, for fifteen years. One of them did a series of scenes with his oppressive father, which he had talked about to this friend many times. When he was through, his friend said, 'I never knew you until now'. What had happened was that he got a different perception of the same person, the same problem: but a changed perception.

DAG: The word 'ecstasy' implies 'to step out of yourself' or 'to give up your individuality' for the honour of the god Dionysus. Through my studies in mythology I came to the conclusion that role reversal is, therefore, an ecstatic experience.

ZERKA: That may be true speaking philosophically, but, emotionally, is it really ecstatic if you role-reverse with someone who is your oppressor? For example, the hostages who came out of Lebanon need to psychodramatize their relationship to their keepers in order to be clear with them. I am not sure that verbal therapy, that is, just talking about it, can do it. The moment you switch from your perspective to the other's perspective and also look upon yourself at the same time, that transitional moment would be the ecstatic experience because you left the point of stasis. I once heard that Wittgenstein said or wrote: 'To learn about the self, step outside the self'.

Psychodramatists working with victims of torture have found that unless these victims reverse roles with their oppressor, they cannot leave behind these reminiscences and the image of the torturer. They are always present. However, when they are able to reverse roles with their torturer and establish tele, so that the torturer becomes a human being instead of an evil image, then these reminiscences and their destructive influences on the victims in the here and now diminish.

Chapter 4

Surplus reality

Psychodramatists often work with surplus reality without taking into account its philosophical perspective. The psychodrama usually starts with the protagonist's problem and during the session the drama goes back to early childhood experiences to heal old wounds. In this case, surplus reality is used as a technique to complete and heal, to have an integrative effect upon the ego so that the protagonist feels better and can get on with his/her life. To bring on stage a dialogue between the protagonist and someone dead or giving him/her a 'new' father or mother are only two examples of this way of using surplus reality.

However, we feel that this orthodox concept and application of surplus reality as a technique to act out fantasies and wishes and, therefore, the ego's needs, is rather restricted and has little to do with the full potential of surplus reality. Surplus reality is more an instrument of disintegration and should be regarded as a theatrical instrument for the director to create discomfort, uneasiness and tensions on stage (Blomkvist and Rützel 1994).

ZERKA: Moreno had this idea of surplus power, taken from Marx's idea of surplus value. He believed that something similar exists in psychodrama. Moreno realized that his protagonists moved into areas which were not real to anyone else but them, and purely subjective. Psychotics are an extreme example of this. These ideas went beyond fantasy, beyond intuition, almost like a trance experience. He recalled Marx's idea of 'surplus value', that what the worker produces results in capital gain by the employer, a surplus which does not belong to the capitalist but should by rights be returned to the workers. Moreno thought surplus reality is 'out there' somewhere and must be made concrete and specific and returned to the centre of the protagonist where it has meaning and purpose. He knew he could not truly meet the psyche of the protagonist unless he lived in the surplus reality together with the protagonist. And he made us, the group members and auxiliary egos, live there as well and helped us live comfortably in our very own surplus reality. Once you tap into a person's psyche, you reach a dimension which is beyond subjective and objective reality. It's a kind of cosmic reality. That's what I really think surplus reality is. It has that timelessness and spacelessness about it that puts us in touch with cosmic powers.

More and more, in the better psychodramas I do, I see myself as a channel, and I get guidance from somewhere, whether it is inspiration, or inspiration and intuition working together in a very specific, focused way. My story about the clown will make that more intelligible. I once had a session with a young man who had a problem with a female superior at work. He said, 'I can never really tell her how I feel about her and about the conflict we have'. I told him, 'The deepest catharsis in psychodrama comes from doing those scenes, those interactions, those moments that do not, cannot, and are not ever likely to happen in life, for whatever reason. So why don't you tell her here?' In order to give him more power and the freedom to do this, I suggested that he step up on his chair. 'Is she a big woman?' He said, 'Yes.' 'Is she taller than you?' 'Yes.' I said, 'Fine. Then step up onto this chair, and you will be bigger and taller.' That gave him the power to really let go; he did, and became quite voluble, spontaneous, and forceful. I'm standing on the floor, my eyes are about on the same level as the pockets in his pants. I'm looking at one pocket and think 'Am I going crazy? I'm hallucinating.' And my inner voice says, 'No, you're not. You're seeing clearly.' And what did I see? A little clown about two and a half or three inches tall, dancing about in his pocket and making funny faces and gestures. A very interesting clown. The protagonist is amusing but doesn't look like a clown. When he finishes his scene and comes down from the chair, he reports that he feels relieved and will try talking to her with more self-confidence. I say to him, 'You know, it's very strange but while you were doing this scene, I saw a clown in you.' Thereupon he caught his breath, sighed profoundly and revealed to us: 'There's a secret in this room. I do clown-therapy in the Children's Hospital.' I did not have that information from him. He had introduced himself as a therapist in a hospital, that was all. This is what I mean by being guided, being a channel, being open and available. It is intuition wedded to inspiration.

DAG: I think it is very important to open one's self up when working with surplus reality. Moreno was also guided when he wrote one of his more important books, *The Words of the Father*. Would you tell us a bit about the circumstances under which this book was written?

ZERKA: I am sure he was in an ecstatic condition. There's no question about that, and he would admit it. Curiously enough, he told me that while he was writing *The Words of the Father* he had no sexual desire whatsoever. His warm-up was in a totally different dimension, in a different state of being. In that state he was hearing voices, not like a mental patient, but hearing voices. And the voices were telling him what to write, and that's what he wrote in red pencil on the walls of an upper room in his castle-like house that had a little tower. The book was published anonymously in 1922. In fact all his German books were published anonymously, including *Das Stegreiftheater* ('Theatre of Spontaneity'), because he believed that creativity is an anonymous category. Everybody is a potential creator. God did not put His name on animals, man did. So Moreno's idea was that the closer we come to God, the more creative we are. And God is also named by man. The Hebrews do not talk about God; one is not allowed to speak His name. It is unspeakable. They are also not allowed to write it out fully. So, if you want to be truly God-like, you are anonymous. That helps you, because your ego disappears, which enables you to merge with the cosmos. By the way, a curious and totally unforeseen side effect of this anonymity was that his German books were not destroyed during the Hitler period since they carried no author's name. After the Second World War Grete Leutz found one of his books in a bookshop in Germany.

The Hebrew language does not write the vowels because they belong to God. These vowels are: i e o u a. If you speak them out they form the name of God: Jehovah.

DAG: What is the relationship between Moreno's God concept and his construction of the psychodrama stage?

ZERKA: First of all, the stage is circular. The little planet on which we live is also circular. Moreno created his own kingdom. He could never be who he was under someone else. That is a 'God-likeness', creating your own little empire. He was lucky to be able to do that and he sacrificed a lot for it. The idea that the stage is circular also means that you learn to control your own world here in action. The metaphor is very clear. Another thing about a circle is that it is total and complete in itself. There's no beginning and no end, speaking in terms of time, for instance. The circle therefore represents wholeness, completion and perfection. Our globe, too, is a three-dimensional circle. So the stage can be considered our globe, a place where we learn to master our own world spontaneously.

I believe an important part in the origin of the psychodrama stage was Moreno's playing with the children in the gardens of Vienna. When he was telling them stories he sat under or on the branch of a tree. A tree has an almost circular shape and the children were sitting around him in a semi-circle, a kind of half-moon. These experiences made a great impression on him as, of course, the Greek theatre has a similar shape.

His original Theatre of Spontaneity was very different; it had a central main stage and several side stages. Later he developed a three level stage, a top concentric stage with two peripheral levels around it. The first level is the reality level, the second the interview level, the third the level of action and where surplus reality is manifested. It has also a balcony for the so-called 'superegos'. Moreno regarded the psychotic patient as living largely in surplus reality. Obviously it is not my reality or yours, it is their subjective reality. Subjective reality can be almost anything, anywhere. You can sit and daydream and then you are in surplus reality – beyond reality.

DAG: Would you please develop the purpose of the different levels of the stage a bit further?

ZERKA: The lowest level is the level of the warm-up. The biggest step is that from being a member of the group into becoming a protagonist: getting up from that chair where you sit among the others, where you were safe, to expose yourself and say: *Mea culpa est*. That is the first level, the warm-up level.

On the middle level you are not yet in action. You are interviewed to get ready for the action level which is the top level of the stage. All the levels actually lead to surplus reality once you step upon them, but you are closer to everyday reality when you first get up. Usually it is not until you have been interviewed and warmed-up into action that you go into surplus reality.

However, there is one distinction, that is if you are asked to soliloquize while walking on the lower level, because this level is more generous and easier to walk on. Then you are already in surplus reality, beyond everyday reality, because in life you do not go around soliloquizing your internal feelings, ideas and emotions, at least not in public where everyone can hear and bear witness.

DAG: Would you say that the director and the protagonist have to distance themselves a little from the group to establish a relationship and that this may be the main function of the second level?

ZERKA: Yes, you are not yet in action, but you are beginning to work together. Another point is that Moreno worked with such a large number of patients who were severely confused; for them he used the second level as a way of introducing the protagonist to the group and to the process without going right into action and it was also a way of saying to the others: 'This is your stage. Any time you feel like coming up and presenting yourself we will sit here together as well.' It is a middle point between being a group member and being a protagonist. It eases the big step from group member to becoming a protagonist by stepping up and being engaged in an interview by the director.

DAG: Would you say that this interview phase on the second level is of a different character than up on the action level?

ZERKA: Yes, it sets the pace for what we are going to be dealing with today. For example, 'What is your main concern? Why are you here?' It sets up the frame. The interview on the action level is for directorial purposes and for deepening and expanding. In the interview we start with the protagonist's concern and in what way it affects that person's life. 'Who is involved in it with you? Can you present that absent person to us by role reversal?' In other words, we begin to expand the situation and explore it in all its dimensions by focusing the interview on the protagonist and his/her world.

DAG: Would you say something about the balcony?

ZERKA: Actually it is a very malleable kind of setting. When earth is presented on stage the balcony can be heaven; when the balcony is earth the stage can be hell or all kinds of levels in between. People very often put deceased persons up on the balcony or their idea of the godhead or the world beyond. Alternatively, it can be used in a very practical way as the balustrade of a bridge when someone wants to commit suicide or as the deck of a ship for a moonlit honeymoon, or romantic type of scene. The balcony is a very flexible instrument and can be used in many different ways. You can travel in the vertical dimension as well as in the horizontal dimension.

DAG: How did the term 'superego' come into psychodrama? It was originally a psychoanalytic term.

ZERKA: 'Superego' as used by Moreno is at variance with that of Freud for whom it was the third level of the ego itself and intrapersonal. For Moreno it meant a heroic role. He observed that heroes are always

> looked up to. They are larger than life and larger than human, like the gods in Greece, living high up on Mount Olympus looking down upon the world. Or think about Hitler, Mussolini, the Royal Family or the Pope. They make sure to appear on a high podium or on a balcony so that people have to look up to them. Thus we bestow on them a more than human, a super-human quality.

Mandala is a Sanskrit word for 'magic circle' and is one of the oldest religious symbols. It is a picture with shapes and figures like squares, triangles, and circles assembled concentrically around a centre. Mandalas are symbols for unity, the self and wholeness. In nature we can discover mandalas in a cell, a spiral nebula, an atom, the solar system, a cobweb, or a snowflake. Man-made mandalas are, for example, the famous rosettes in the medieval cathedrals, the Yin and Yang, the pentagram. A mandala is an image of the universe: it constantly grows out of a centre and tends towards the periphery and, at the same time, converges from diversity towards the centre.

The centre is a point, an abstract concept, which itself has no dimension. Expanding it into the second dimension we come to the circle, which in the third dimension becomes a ball. If we now add the next dimension, time, we come to the creation of the universe, or, as the Native Americans say, the world of Maya. If we take away space and time, which are only an illusion for the Native American Indians, then the whole universe collapses into its primary centre point. This central point, which in a material way does not exist, is common to all mandalas; in it all opposites meet and polarity ceases to exist. It is like the hub of a turning wheel which itself stands still.

We can find similar ideas relating to the stage's centre and periphery in J.L. Moreno's book The Theatre of Spontaneity, *published in Germany in 1924 as* Das Stegreiftheater, *in which he wrote the following:*

> *When I entered a theatre I knew that it had moved far astray from its primordial form. Therefore, after I had constructed a stage for the new theatre which was to give mankind a sort of dramatic religion, many asked by whom I had been influenced to build a stage of such dimensions, one which is placed in the center instead of the periphery; one which permits movement unlimited instead of limited; one which is open to all sides instead of in front; one which has the whole community around it, instead of only a part; one which has the form of a circle instead of a square; one which moves up in vertical dimension, instead of maintaining a single level. The stimulus was*

> *not the stage of Shakespeare or the stage of the Greeks, I had taken the model from nature itself.*
>
> *(J.L. Moreno 1973: 4)*

Another definition of the psychodrama stage is given in an article by Leif Dag Blomkvist and Thomas Rützel in which they wrote the following:

> *On the psychodrama stage there is no differentiation of time at all. There is also no differentiation of different kinds of realities with one regarded as more real, valid or true than another. Surplus reality can be defined as an intersection between different realities, known and unknown, where the ego's ability to control and distinguish ceases. This state determines ecstasy, which we understand from its etymological root to be 'leaving the limits of one's individuality'. This is a state in which one does not experience things as one used to, but looks upon them from another unfamiliar perspective. This perspective can either belong to an unknown part of the self, to another person, known or unknown, or to an impersonal force.*
>
> *(Blomkvist and Rützel 1994: 235)*

Chapter 5

Clinical applications: the use of humour and magic objects

Zerka T. Moreno

Moreno wanted to be remembered as 'The Man who Brought Joy and Laughter into Psychiatry'. He told me this before he died and it is engraved upon his tombstone. The idea of having laughter and joy imported into what is generally regarded as such serious business may strike some people unpleasantly and perhaps make them feel we are being frivolous and therefore denigrating our counselees. However, laughter, when appropriately applied, may bring relief from what is often a stressful situation and create a space where objective distance can be achieved. It is not meant to turn a tragic situation into a nonsensical one, but to cast a new light upon it which in turn can facilitate an entirely new response and attitude.

Finding a magic object and inserting it as a tool of healing is implicit in all improvisational theatre and one has only to recall its effect when seeing a gifted mime, such as Marcel Marceau, produce one with great ease and grace, out of thin air. It propels us into the realm of wonder and surprise.

The following cases present the application of humour and of magic objects to enable the protagonist to find new strength, creativity and integration.

The client is a young woman of 22, an actor. The presenting problem is her father's depressiveness. For the last 12 years he has threatened to commit suicide. Her mother divorced him and has remarried happily. He claims she is the only woman he ever loved and cannot forgive her for deserting him. The client, whom I will call Naomi, is the only child of this marriage.

Naomi sets the scene, a corner of the kitchen where she cooks their meal; she suspects he does not eat properly as he has lost a good deal of weight over the years and his depression is pervasive. She role-reverses into her father's being and is interviewed in that role. It is clear that his life is useless to him, he just goes through the motions in a robot-like manner. Returned to her own role, Naomi picks an auxiliary ego to represent her father and the scene begins. It soon becomes evident that no matter what argument she brings to the situation, Naomi is unable to get through his wall of misery. He sounds extremely righteous and declares that Naomi's mother is the carrier of the blame. He just wants to die.

Naomi looks helplessly at me, raises her shoulders and hands and says: 'You see, that is exactly how he is. It's hopeless and I get so angry at him that whatever love I have for him just melts away. But he is a loving father and I am so sorry for him. The fact is that his depression drove my mother away from him. Now he has no one in the world but me. He makes no effort to find other connections. So I can't really get angry at him.'

Encouraged by me to try it here, she shakes her head, starts to weep and says: 'I can't, not even here'. I let her cry, comfort her so she can let it out. When she stops weeping and is calm again, I dismiss her auxiliary and ask her to role reverse and be her father.

Now I interview him again, and commiserate with him, tell him that indeed his life is totally useless. Then, as she relaxes into the role more and more, I recall that this scenario has gone on long before the marriage and subsequent divorce and that Naomi is dealing with 'the dead hand of history'. Going totally zany into surplus reality (remember Magritte's painting of a pipe with the statement *Ceci n'est pas une pipe* – 'This is not a pipe' – meaning it is only the depiction of a pipe) I realize that this is the depiction of a misery but is it truly misery? So I say to him: 'I understand you want to die. Would you like to die eating strawberries?' Naomi is taken completely by surprise and starts to laugh and laugh and laugh, which breaks the spell.

When Naomi has calmed down again, I suggest that she return to her own role with this awareness that her father has been playing on her sympathy for him for 12 years and that none of her interventions with him can sway him from that path. Logic makes absolutely no sense to him. Next I propose that she redo the scene with the same auxiliary ego whom I instruct not to turn away from his martyr role. Her task is not to fight him any longer, but to agree with him in whatever argument he brings to bear. We are experimenting, of course, with a new response to an old situation, guiding her into a spontaneous reaction that has no relation to the past.

Now we watch as Naomi relaxes and tries to keep a straight face; she responds to each of his challenges with a calm: 'Yes of course. You're right, Dad. I see just what you mean', etc.

The point is that Naomi had been certain that her father would commit suicide and that it was her job to turn him away from it. Once she grasped that this was not part of his plan or else he would have done it long ago, she could begin to see how she had been enmeshed. Being helped to 'laugh' her way out of that net she could begin to handle both herself and her father in a new way.

The auxiliary ego shared that the new way was somehow soothing to him; he did not have to strive so hard to convince her of the depth of his misery and that lightened his burden. He was heard and supported, not persuaded to change.

Naomi is instructed to carry out this different way of dealing with her father in life itself. She subsequently reported that, indeed, he began to lighten up with her and eventually to admit that perhaps he had exaggerated his misery. It was as if when she found this new contact with him, not as an adversary but as a comrade in arms, he could let go of some of the past and be more completely in the present. She was slowly able to assist him in overcoming some of his unfinished business with her mother. I also explained that this in no way diminished her loyalty to her mother.

You may ask: 'How did you, Zerka, get hold of this crazy question: "Would you like to die eating strawberries?"' It is a case of active imagination on the part of the therapist, a stepping out of a small, tight, no-exit corner and dancing around in the larger world to find a surprise. Years before, I had seen a not very meaningful but funny movie with Eddie Cantor called *The Kid from Spain*. The story line was very wacky and when the protagonist, here Eddie, is faced with the threat of death by a number of crooks who are making him pay for some misdeed committed by his father, now dead, he is told: 'Get wise, you are going to die but you can choose your last meal. So what do you want to eat?' Eddie's response is 'I would like to die eating strawberries'. He is told in no uncertain terms that 'They are not in season', whereupon Eddie answers: 'I can wait'.

It was not only my question which struck me as way out, it was in the back of my mind that 'I can wait' was the issue here. And waiting was what Naomi's father was good at: waiting for death but also waiting for someone to help him out of his 'vortex of misery'.

How does one teach students active, creative imagination? Perhaps by allowing them to find their own lunatic fringes in such a way as to help them fit the punishment to the crime, so to speak. That is where surplus reality is at the service of the therapist. One is not really *being* lunatic, just playing in that sphere.

My second case illustrates how the use of a magic object may produce a leap into surplus reality to the benefit of the protagonist.

A 30-year-old woman, an academic at a university, presents herself with her life-long problem: feeling markedly inferior in every respect to her beautiful and talented mother, an opera star. One visible aspect of this burden is Laura's physical bearing. She stands and sits with her head down, her neck bowed like a nicked Easter lily. Even when engaged in the interview with me, this stance does not change a great deal. Her back is never really straight. Laura is asked to set up a scene with her mother which will show us her typical interactions with this imposing woman. It becomes clear that she still feels like a shy 7-year-old in her presence, looking up to her mother on her Olympian heights. When asked to soliloquize about her feelings, she blurts out: 'I used to be able to sing and enjoy my voice but after having heard you, it is impossible for me to lift mine. And now, at the university, when I am teaching, I am aware that my speaking voice is becoming affected and students may not be able to hear me.'

To me, this reduced voice requires some immediate intervention. I first enquire if there is a medical or physical reason for this phenomenon. Laura admits she has often asked herself that and had it checked: results were negative. Long-term contact with Laura is not practical; she lives far away and has come to see me during her vacation, having been urged to do so by a close friend. Observing her pride in her status as an academic when she introduced herself, it strikes me that a 7-year-old would just about begin to appreciate the use of a ruler. You will note that our interpretations come out of the client's performance; they may not always be spoken out loud, we just put them into action. I must admit that these connections are not always made consciously but on some subliminal level. They often do not become clear to me until after the fact. I ask Laura to stand as straight as she can because I need to give her a remedy. She cooperates well and lifts her head higher. When asked to close her eyes and open her mouth, she obeyed meekly. Remember that when we are ill and requiring a remedy in childhood, it is often given to us orally. I did not, however, interpret this to her, but put my interpretation into immediate action. She learned about her mother's talents about the age of 7 and was deeply impressed by her singing. Up until then singing had been a delightful pastime for her. Then she was robbed of that way of expressing her joy. Now that 7-year-old is about to be healed.

I tell Laura that I am giving her a 'magic ruler', one that is soft and very pliable, soothing to the throat and chest; it is going to help her not only to straighten up, but to open her chest, allowing air to be inhaled and exhaled freely. I am nourishing a deprived body part, her vocal tract. By putting in something soothing, she will be enabled to put out something soothing. I suggest to her that she allow the remedy to enter her and when it is all inside her, to swallow. She is good at following these suggestions: suggestibility is a profound aspect of Laura's character, as we saw from her first scene. When she has swallowed a few times, I ask her to hold up her head slowly and in a comfortable position and to feel the strength which the magic ruler has bestowed upon her, including making it possible to keep her head up, her shoulders relaxed, her chest wide open. She does as she is asked. When ready, she lifts her eyelids to reveal glowing eyes.

Asked if she could feel that lovely, soft, pliable strength in her, she nods, yes. 'What do you want to sing now? I know you can do it, perhaps not the way your mother does, but in your own way.' Laura thinks for a moment and says: 'I remember applying to sing in the madrigal choir at school; I was turned down, but I know several madrigals because I used to sit in a corner and listen to the choir, hoping I could sing them one day.' 'Do it now and let us enjoy it together', thereby correcting two traumatic events in one.

Laura lifts her voice which is sweet and clear; she sings to her heart's content. It would be hard to convey the tears of joy that follow her performance, and the pleasure she had given us and herself.

Magic and surplus reality are in the same realm. Moreno declared that spontaneity–creativity, the twin principle, is the basis of our work. Using the twins by returning to our primordial source where everything is possible, we are transported into the magic realm which can heal us. We must not forget those primordial sources of our humanity, but trust them as does the child. Reviving the trusting child, the one before the trauma, is often the essence of healing. This brings us back to Moreno's playing with the children in the gardens of Vienna. He described it in *Psychodrama: First Volume*, as 'The Kingdom of the Children', a magic realm he did not ever want to leave. Returning to these roots brings us to surplus reality.

I use a different magic object in the third example. A young man, Brian, offers himself as protagonist in a very large gathering, with his concern that at age 32 he is unable to find the woman life-partner he has been searching for. He admits that he does not allow himself to make that final commitment; he knows it is tied in with his mother and her death. Asked how old he was when she died he tells us he was 14. When he is asked if he was present at her death, he almost starts to cry and is barely able to whisper: 'Yes'. Now he sets the scene. He and his mother are mountain climbing. Both of them are excellent, experienced climbers, but in spite of that his mother loses her foothold and plunges to her death. Brian blames himself for not having been able to save her. The tension in the group is palpable. It is clear that the identification with Brian is very profound.

I suggest he tell his mother, embodied by a chosen auxiliary ego who is lying still on the ground, what he was unable to convey to her in life and how it has haunted him all these years. She was a good mother and he loved her dearly. Brian kneels by her side and tells her of this terrible sorrow and his feelings of guilt and remorse these past 18 years. He asks for forgiveness for failing to save her life. The auxiliary ego is also crying and tells him that she has forgiven him long ago because no one could have saved her and he should no longer carry that burden. She gives him permission to find his life's companion. He is not to blame and has every right to be happy. They embrace and cry together until he becomes calm. Then I suggest that he let her go in peace, whereupon the auxiliary ego rises, stands up, walks away, making her exit behind the group through the door while Brian watches her quietly. (We always have someone go and retrieve the auxiliary ego and bring that person back into the group after having had a chance to shed the role.)

My sense is that this is not yet sufficient release for Brian. He is still profoundly attached to his mother. I tell him that these past 18 years of burden constitute a very long emotional umbilical cord to his mother. (Remember that the cord of the climber did not hold her.) Now that she and he are at rest with each other it is time to unwind and cut it. He leaps off the imaginary mountain and runs downhill, starting to unwind the cord from his navel. I encourage him not to rush it, to take as long as 18 years of binding him need to unwind. Then, when he stops, I toss him a pair of 'magic scissors'. Brian catches them and cuts the cord. Then I recommend that he give the cord a loving burial as he and his mother had a loving connection. He digs with his hands, creates a nice deep hollow, gently lifts the cord and puts it in, covers it with earth, pats it lovingly, resting there for a few minutes.

When he returns to the group we just silently join him in a group hug. No words are spoken. Sometimes only silence is appropriate. Brian leaves us, holding his head high, his face relaxed. I have no doubt that whatever his future brings him, he can face it differently.

I have since used these magic scissors a number of times and they have never failed me or the protagonist. I routinely ask the protagonist to please return them to me as they may be needed by others.

There are many ways we can produce magic objects as they are required and surplus reality technique brings us to new levels of experiencing ourselves in the world.

Chapter 6

The surreal experience

'The surreal experience' is a term used by the surrealists but which could also be of much value in psychotherapy and psychodrama. It could be regarded as a moment of transition where beginning and end are the same thing. This moment of transition is characterized by the feeling of estrangement and the act of waiting and expecting. What was familiar earlier now becomes unfamiliar and strange. The reality widens, which is also the Morenian description of surplus reality. The word 'wide' derives from the Indo-Germanic word 'ui-itos'*, meaning, in German,* auseinandergegangen. *There is no equivalent in English for this German word but a literal translation could be 'one departed from one another', or, in other terms, 'to fall to pieces'. Surplus reality, seen from this perspective, leads to disintegration or falling to pieces.*

> *Waiting above all implies that something is missing, something for which one is waiting. However, that which is missing at the same time fills the act of waiting with significant content, turning the feeling of absence into its opposite.*
>
> *(Sjölin 1981: 407)*

This moment of unclarity was something the surrealists looked upon in two divergent ways: one embraces waiting as a desirable precondition and a driving force for discoveries, the other associates waiting with restraint and total availability.

DAG: Do you think as psychodramatists we try to relieve the pain of our patients too fast and try to come to a solution too quickly? Wouldn't it be purposeful for the drama to encourage the patient or protagonist to experience suffering and patience?

ZERKA: Moreno sometimes explained psychodrama as a small injection of insanity under conditions of control. When challenged about the dangers of such a procedure his response was: 'I am not so much concerned with the insanity, but I am concerned about the control. If the patient would do what is done in the theatre on the outside, in the world at large, that could well be dangerous to the patient as well as to others. In psychodrama the patient can both do it and learn control from it.' The psychodrama theatre should empower the protagonist to experience the insanity in a non-threatening situation and in one in which control can be gained.

Once I was dealing with an apparently suicidal patient. I sensed that she was playing with the suicide, and that she did not really intend to do it. My impression was confirmed when she declared during the psychodrama that she would commit suicide by taking three pills of Valium. This did not strike me as genuine. I encouraged the protagonist to take more pills. And she answered, 'Then I take four pills.' 'Well, one cannot die from taking four pills either.' I encouraged her to take something poisonous so she could encounter true suffering and the pain of death intensely. The woman became more and more resistant to facing her suicide and death. I was moving her towards the suffering and went into surplus reality, I went beyond reality to be able to give her that experience. I did not want to solve her problems. What she needed was to go through the experience of suicide without the pressure of doing it in life, in reality. I evaluated her need as a cry for help, so the next scene was one in which the person she loved the most came to her bedside and declared his love and need for her.

There was a wonderful Beatles song in the 60s which was called 'Let It Be' and relates to the idea of waiting, of sinking into the experience, of flowing with the moment. It has a meaning in itself – almost Zen.[1] The surreal experience is an existential one.

When I first came to America and was very lonely, on hot nights I used to go to Riverside Drive in Manhattan, New York. I would stand up above and look down on Riverside Drive, and there would be masses of cars coming and going on the road. I said to myself, 'Look at them; they've all got somewhere to go; I've got no place to go. Nobody knows I'm here. I feel like a piece of flotsam on the ocean, totally without roots. What am I doing here?' It was a very painful time. Everybody else in this world seemed to me to have a goal; they were driving somewhere. I was not going anywhere. Looking back now, I value that experience enormously, though it was very painful at the time. This experience felt very real. I had no roots; I had left Europe, and had not yet rooted here. I was like a piece of flotsam. It was an existential truth, painful and agonizing as it was.

DAG: Is it good for a person so lonely to feel like flotsam?

ZERKA: At the time, it was terrible, frightful agony. Many of us have experienced it at one time or another. It isn't always as graphic as I showed you just now. But it is also the realization on some level that one is all alone in this world. That is the truth. One is basically alone. One meets a few meaningful people along the way. We are born alone; we die alone. And that is existentially the way it is. So this is a slice of life that I had better make my peace with. Well, I found it very instructive, painful as it was.

DAG: So you would say that knowing you are born alone and die alone, and encountering that loneliness is part of a full catharsis, to be able to take that condition spontaneously?

ZERKA: Yes. And that prepared me to write a poem when I listened to the record *The Words of the Father* for the first time after Moreno's death. Let me read the poem to you.

What shall I say
of death
when man's technology
restores your voice?
I hear it, disbelieving,
in deep shock
and realize your presence
in great pain.
I weep
and weep again.
My loss is sharp, is here,
in being, now,
alone.
Your voice is real,
yet gone.
Your spirit's immortality
a painful newness brings.
I cannot bear it.
Tears are not enough,
I want to stay and yet
to run away.
The telephone's ring

breaks through my spell.
I answer it and weep,
no longer keep it
secret.

In the dark
we share our sorrow
Dee and I.
She knows and stands me by,
along the wire
another man-made thing.

In writing this
again in agony I mourn
and sob and moan
as I have never done before,
in animal intensity
which grips and seizes me.

Is this **my** voice?
It has an unfamiliar sound
yet universal.
I realize: This is
the morning of my
mourning,
the living of my loss
and that of all the world's,
the 'Farewells' still unsaid,
unspoken.
Across the years
my link with you remains,
unbroken.
I need the comfort of my tears.

You who have given me
my life anew,
again and again,
Oh God, how many times?
And also ripped my guts
with pain.

Last night
my students shared lovingly.
They had no fears,
they stood around,
they sensed your presence,
very near.
Ann held me
in her comforting embrace
and wept with me,
as did they all.
Some wiped my face.
Meinolf supplied a handkerchief,
all new, a virgin cloth,
for me to blow my nose,
absorb the tears.
And Jannika in privacy revealed
she saw tonight
a fog at edge of Hessian Lake.
We'd wandered there together,
the group and I.

This fog contained a shadow
which hovered
at my side.
She thought it might
be you.
I did not see or feel you there.
I needed this, your voice,
to have you close,
once more reliving
our first journey in 1941.
Your voice, dynamic, young
and ringing, there
in the Pullman car,
presenting then these very Words,
a gift, only to me.
The railroad's roar
mingling in
my ear's delight,
the galleys of your book
spread on the seats,

your giant hands,
your eyes, your presence,
reading, only to me,
out loud,
with Stentor's voice.
How do I convey
the singing in my soul
when it joined yours?

There simply is no way.

Before you died
I promised
you would never lose me.
'I'll find you again',
I said.
You heard, nodded, gave sign
that you approved.
But there is no
limit for all this
in time.
Now I must live
while you are so removed.
My life still runs its course
full charged with loving.

Who knows what oceans
I must cross,
what lives touch,
what companions meet and
cherish yet,
before I once again
am there with you?

The cosmos is our home
and no one shall be
there
alone.

(Z. Moreno 1993)

ZERKA: I believe that in the cosmos we are not alone. We are part of some large cosmic 'whatever-it-is', a network, a web, but we're not alone. We are alone here, yes, and can be lonely. That is not true in the cosmos at large. Do you remember what Goethe said, *Einsam bin ich, nicht alleine* ('I am lonely, not alone')? One can be lonely and not alone. So my experience at Riverside Drive was one of loneliness, as well as aloneness. And everybody with some sensibility has experienced something like that.

DAG: Did J.L. Moreno use a lot of surplus reality on stage?

ZERKA: When a patient came to him and said that he was Jesus Christ, he said, 'Of course. Jesus, how wonderful. I've always wanted to meet you. Show me what your life is like. I really want to get to know you. Take me into your life, into your world.'

DAG: When you saw J.L. Moreno doing that, what were your thoughts?

ZERKA: 'How does he dare to do this? This is scary as hell! But he feels so confident; he must know what he's doing. I'm never going to be able to do psychodrama. I'm *never* going to be a director; I'll *never* know enough, I'll *never* be wise enough. I'll *never* be great enough. I'll just learn to be the best ever auxiliary ego.' Yet, here I am, a director of psychodrama. So one really develops. It is important to realize that Moreno dealt with some very severely disturbed psychotic and neurotic patients. So, being young and vulnerable and what I consider fairly ignorant of psychiatric matters, not yet very well schooled, this was not what I had been taught life was about. However, I have an older sister who had been psychotic. Through her I learned a lot about psychotic breakdowns.

I remember a psychologist saying to J.L., 'Moreno, I hope one day to be able to do what you do, which is to reach a gentle hand into the psyche and bring it out lovingly, with care and with skill and with courage. I hope to be able to do that.'

DAG: Zerka, would you please describe a bit how you and J.L. Moreno used surplus reality? Would you please develop that a bit further?

ZERKA: I should like to refer first to two levels of reality: subjective and objective reality. Usually, in objective reality, you and I can agree on what's happening here: we're in this room, there are two beds, there is a table, a typewriter, etc.

When the psychotic enters the picture, all that does not matter. There is no reality to this space. The internal is all that matters. And sometimes it is even vice versa so that the internal becomes the external. So, where are we? Whose reality are we talking about? Obviously, it is deeper, wider and broader than anything else that you and I can see or hear or touch. It is beyond all that. It is just as real for that psychotic, or even more real than you and me; we are just artefacts in this world; we are not real.

This split between objective and subjective reality has its seeds in childhood. Moreno could see the child in a person very clearly. He was a paediatrician before he became a psychiatrist. Although the child is in interaction with others from birth on and learns a great deal about its world in this manner, in the first few months of life the child is only aware of itself. It experiences itself as the centre of the universe. It is still in the matrix of all-identity. It is the centre of the universe; it *is* the universe (J.L. Moreno 1977).

At some point, as the neuro-physiological structures begin to develop and as there are emotional or physical traumata, the child begins to realize that it is not alone and also not in full control of its environment. It hits itself against the side of the crib and that hurts. It has a stomach ache or a fever, and Mummy doesn't know what to do about it.

Every human being experiences this split; it is universal, this split between subjective and objective reality. Insofar as objective reality is non-nourishing, non-nurturing, the child withdraws and returns to that subjective reality where it is once more totally in control. If that is repeated again and again, if there is no bridge between these two levels of reality, there can sprout the seedlings for the psychotic experience, the drug experience, the criminal experience, the addictive experience, because we want to believe that we are totally in control.

So, for Moreno, psychodrama is the bridge between these two levels of reality. If that means going into the total subjectivity of that person, that is what you do, and that is what treating psychotics is about. Having had the opportunity to live through these experiences, it may enable the psychotic to give them up and re-enter the world of objective reality (Moreno and Moreno 1975b).

Without this treatment many criminals project the image of being totally in control onto the outer world. So they cannot admit that they are not in control. They somehow know they are not, and yet they act as if they are while fearing they might get caught. Many of them do get caught; but a certain number do not. As to psychotics, those who recover by themselves, we assume they use some internal near-psychodramatic techniques to come out of the psychotic world.

There was an example in Colorado some years ago where they brought hardcore juvenile delinquents to the electric chair-room, giving them a crude 'psychodramatic shock'. And in every group they took there the youngsters were told by the corrections officer, 'If you continue this life, this is where you will end.' And again in every group they brought, at least one boy said, 'That's right, that's where I will end.' It seems that they *know* better, but they can't *do* better.

Chapter 7

Psychodrama and the deliberately distorted mirror technique

The mirror technique is one in which the protagonist is taken from the stage and replaced by a group member who takes his/her role in the selected scene. The protagonist looks upon the action. The purpose of using this technique is to enable the protagonist not to be personally involved in the action, that he/she should see the whole situation from a distant perspective rather than an involved, individual point of view.

The method of separating the actor from the role to create a distance between the role, the masque and the actor, is ancient and often used in the Chinese theatre and is there in fact called the 'distance technique'. In Europe it was particularly developed by Bertolt Brecht, with the so-called technique of estrangement. The audience should not feel into the different characters' personal feelings as is the case in the Stanislavski tradition. On the contrary, the created estrangement should activate the audience to see an objective and historical perspective in the situation. This use of the technique of estrangement goes against the theatrical tradition inherited from Aristotle who believed that the cathartic effect or the purification of emotions lay in the personal involvement with the different characters in the play, which means catharsis came through a process of identification.

DAG: Tell me something about the mirror technique and in which way you and J.L. Moreno used it.

ZERKA: The interesting thing about the mirror, especially when we are children standing in front of it trying to comb our hair or dress ourselves, is that stupid person in the mirror who doesn't know how to do it right. The mirror image is a negative image, not a positive one. So, we have to be careful when we use the mirror technique.

Moreno often did it to shock the protagonist into a new realization, to give that person a challenge: 'Is this really what you are like, is this what your world looks like?' We often exaggerated the mirror image, using techniques of deliberate distortion. Moreno instructed the auxiliary ego to exaggerate the behaviour of the protagonist to a degree beyond reality. In that sense it was a surplus reality technique. He called it the 'deliberately distorted mirror technique'. Its purpose was to challenge the protagonist. However, the importance of the technique was that we gave the protagonist an opportunity to correct the mirror, both for face-saving and for self-healing reasons. 'How would you like this mirror of yourself to be, how should it be, how would it be good for you?'

Moreno and I made some interesting observations when this technique was used on psychopaths. They go back to the same psychopathic pattern; they cannot change the mirror. It is frozen. For us the image created on the stage is a negative image; for them, it is *the* image, and they are unable to change it, or unable to recognize it as their own. Or they deny any relationship to this image.

DAG: What do you mean by psychopathic pattern?

ZERKA: There is a curious coldness about psychopaths in relation to themselves and others. They know how to seek out one's vulnerable spots, they will use them, they will play with them and extract what they want. They feel very little sense of obligation about it. But I don't think they are totally without a sense of superego because when they are put into a relevant role reversal, facing themselves, they are capable of seeing their failings and can be harshly critical. At least, that has been my experience with a number I have directed.

I would like to talk about tele for a moment. I like to think of tele as 'liking and loving in one'. Very often we love someone, but we don't like him/her or vice versa. For full tele, the two must flow together. The liking is an appreciation of the other; the loving is seeing him/her with faults and failings and still loving and seeing the beauty in that person. That, I think, is perhaps something that the psychopath does not experience: the beauty part. They can access you but it is mostly in a cold manner and without any deeper feeling.

However, I once did a session with a young man of age 18 in a mental hospital in the Midwest who, by his own admission, was adopted into a family that was good to him and well educated. He had everything he wanted. He was sent to a Catholic school and was kicked out for misbehaving in every way. In the hospital he was told that if he did not snap out of this he would end up in prison. I decided that in the psychodrama I would turn him into God and that I would take his part because there were no auxiliary egos available. He was considered a hardcore delinquent by the staff, a very troublesome and troubled young man. I put him up on stage and I knelt in front of him and said: 'God, I need your help.' He pulled himself up to his 6-foot height and looked down at me and said, 'I have nothing to give you. I have given you seven chances and you have muffed them all.' In his role I pleaded: 'But God, you are a God of Love.' 'Not for you!' Then I responded: 'But how can I go through life without your love?' His prescription to me in his role was: 'You will have to find it within yourself.' And that was the end of the session.

So one cannot say that he was not aware of what he was doing. 'Don't come to me for affection or love. Find it in yourself.' Here was a turning point in this young man's evaluation of the self. He realized what he failed to be doing for himself. For me this was a revelation. This guy knows very well what he is doing, he just does not know what or whom to love, doesn't know how to come forth with love for himself.

Such persons need help to change their self-image. They need help to learn to trust someone. Many of them have been bashed about to the point where they do not trust anyone any more, and thus they are confirmed in their perception that the world is principally a bad place.

A statement Moreno used to make is: 'When the child comes into the world and assesses the world around itself it questions: "Is the universe friendly?"' Unfortunately we have to say for many: No! There is very limited friendliness in this world for many children, sad to say, but they do not all become hardcore delinquents. Those who do did not achieve that by themselves. Many have been seriously mishandled. Therefore, I cannot say with certainty that psychopaths do not have insight or superego. Many of us are unable to reach such a person. That would be the honest thing to admit. But to classify someone as untreatable is, in my opinion, a crime. It would be better to say: 'I cannot treat this person, but someone else may be able to.' Therapists have to try and help these people, to show them that there is still hope and beauty in the world. We have to deepen the tele and expand the soul. I know it is very hard because there is so much violence and callousness in our world. Besides, they are very complicated and often threatening to work with. It may be our fear of them that makes us impotent in dealing with them. And, of course, patients have killed therapists.

DAG: Would you say that what Moreno did was to encourage exaggeration of a protagonist's presentation up to a point where it became distorted, something we would call 'maximizing' today?

ZERKA: If that was called for, depending on what the problem was. In the mirror technique, when a group member has taken the role of the protagonist, the latter is, on one hand, the one who is up on the stage, and on the other hand, the observer removed from the stage looking at the scene; the protagonist is now equally a member of the group. So we are creating a split. Since the image is created by another group member acting in the role of the protagonist this negative image is not necessarily experienced by the protagonist as his/hers any longer. The protagonist somehow looks upon the scene with the eye of a group member. As an observer s/he is removed from the mirroring process and thus can regard the scene as something not directly related to him/her. The picture can become a profoundly positive one by changing it. On some level, it is unlike the glass mirror; it goes beyond the glass mirror and becomes, therefore, surplus reality.

DAG: The mirror from a physiological point of view reverses things or puts them upside down, it perverts the image. 'Perverse' is a Latin word and means 'to go back; to turn around; to destroy'. However, in the 15th century it was used in the context of going against the will of God.

If the mirror technique in psychodrama should be considered from a mythological point of view, the psychodrama director would have to turn around the scene or turn it upside down. S/he must deliberately distort rather than use the mirror technique in the usual way of taking the protagonist out of the scene. This brings the protagonist to a point where s/he sees himself reflected in the perverse perspective. The psychodramatic mirror image leads the protagonist into a surreal dimension to which s/he will react. One could say that s/he is now acting from the perspective of the shadow and thus looks upon him-/herself from that perspective. As a rule the protagonist will react with great resistance to this deliberate distortion.

However, the perspective of the perverse must ignore the normal reaction. Usual comments from protagonists are: 'But I did say that my mother and father were always fighting. So why am I then playing loving and caring parents? This is perverse.' Or another example: 'I told you that my husband always starts a fight with me and not vice versa. Up to this day I never raised my voice to anybody. Is it therapeutic that I should go around playing a screaming bitch?' These comments show the technique's *moment of surprise*.

ZERKA: You have to be creative in directing psychodrama. Moreno taught us to be comfortable with our own lunatic fringes. I think one of the reasons people are afraid of directing psychodramas is because they are afraid of their own fantasies. They have not yet learned to be protagonist enough to deal and play with their own lunatic fringes. That's what makes them fearful; they have not become familiar with their own craziness and therefore have not learned to trust it. Moreno said that madness is often the source of great creativity.

DAG: You see yourself as a medium who is guided by something or someone. However, very often directors do not trust such guidance. Spontaneity then turns into anxiety, so directors run aground in their directing.

ZERKA: Directors seem to hesitate in trusting their guidance, whether it comes as a hunch or an intuition. I think many of them are just too cerebral. They use their brain too much. What seems to help me in my directing is to be naive – not to know too much.

Psychodrama is essentially a combination of science and art. If the art is not there, you may have poor science as well. I was delighted recently by an article in an issue of MIT's *Technology Review* by Samuel C. Florman in which he stated: 'Even today, engineers agree that intuition, practical experience and artistic sensibility are at least as important in their work as is the application of scientific theory' (Florman 1997: 59). Or, in an issue of *Parabola* dealing with the geometry of the labyrinth: 'There is a definite path and a method that must be followed to the end, but sometimes to understand it fully or wholly, we must investigate the validity of a complementary path or of the same path presented differently' (Conty 1992: 14). These positions reflect our own. Einstein never did any experiments; it was all in his mind, in his imagination, in his searching. He did not need the experiments. He is also known to have said, 'Imagination is more important than knowledge.' That is not to say he never made mistakes; we all make mistakes. I try to give the protagonist the space to correct me if I am off the mark.

Cerebral psychodrama is dry and dusty; it does not please. On the other hand, what appears to be totally spontaneous psychodrama may be chaotic and may not lead anywhere, it can be Dada.[1] It is not really spontaneous either; it is just going over the borders. Even surplus reality has its borders. It does not just overflow; it has its shapes and its forms, its tempi and its rhythm.

Moreno would probably be considered a surrealist in many ways. We can not fix the creative geniuses into a frame. They are their own frame, and their own beacon.[2]

Albert Einstein also held some deeply rooted religious beliefs which he expressed in German in the following words:

> *Das kosmische Erlebnis der Religion ist das stärkste und edelste Motiv naturwissenschaftlicher Forschung.*
> *Das tiefste und erhabenste Gefühl, dessen wir fähig sind, ist das Erlebnis der Mystik. Aus ihm allein keimt wahre Wissenschaft.*[3]
>
> *(Einstein 1984: 194)*

DAG: Are you a surrealist, Zerka?

ZERKA: You tell me. You're better able to judge than I am, because you've seen my directing. I cannot judge my own directing that well.

DAG: I think you are a surrealist. You were the one who inspired and influenced me in my studies in surrealism and surplus reality.

Talking about being one's own beacon, I remember a story I would like to share. When I was a student at the Moreno Institute in Beacon you directed a psychodrama with a male protagonist. This experience influenced my whole style as a psychodrama director, both in a practical and in a philosophical sense. The protagonist was concerned with his divorce and to whom the children would be granted custody. It was a touching psychodrama. However, the man constantly forgot the names, ages and sexes of his three children. Everybody started to feel uncomfortable and questioned the truth and reality of the production, but the drama and acting out continued.

At a certain point he stopped the drama and confessed that he had neither a wife nor children, and that he lived a very lonely life. Whereas the group was shocked by his confession, you were not. You did not regard this production as a lie but rather as a psychodramatic truth. This truth is free from the boundaries of reality – some kind of an existential truth. In surplus reality a lie can become truth, the Creator can be born.

ZERKA: Those were his children. That was real for him. One has to respect that. They were his creations. These creations probably made his everyday life bearable.

DAG: How did you build up such a respect?

ZERKA: I think as I grew older, I became more humble. Recently I was asked in what way I had changed most as a director. I have become less and less directive and more Zen, non-judgemental, everything goes; on some level everything is acceptable.

I did respect his creativity and his honesty about it. That psychodrama took place more than twenty years ago so I must have had this attitude even then. Perhaps it has to do with my training with psychotic patients.

This reminds me of an oriental story that fits this kind of situation. There was a guru who had 25 disciples. Among them was one person who stole and lied and cheated the others. The others came to the guru and said, 'How can you permit this man to be in our midst? He lies and he steals and cheats. We do not understand how you can permit this.' The guru replied, 'But do you not see, you're already there, you already know it is wrong; he is not there yet. Should I shut him out because he is not already there?'

About this man who did not have a wife or children, I may have thought, 'He is not there, but in his mind he is there'. Is that not reasonable to accept? They are more real to him in some way than anything else – these children, his creations. If you do not let him have them, how is he ever going to free himself of them? These ideas are going to continue to control him indefinitely.

DAG: I think you and J.L. Moreno revolutionized the world through psychodrama. In the treatment of psychosis you did not confront the patient's psychotic reality with the reality of his or her environment. Instead you let the patient act on the stage and made role reversals with the persons and figures of his/her world. The purpose was to build up relations to this world and, therefore, to build up tele. In his report 'The Psychodrama of Adolf Hitler' (Moreno and Moreno 1975a), a psychodrama that took place early in World War II, Moreno describes a patient who was convinced he was the real Adolf Hitler whereas the Hitler in Germany was an impostor. Moreno treated this man with psychodrama and let him act out his reality. When the man felt better Moreno asked him what caused these ideas. The man said that since he was a young boy he had the dream of conquering the world and destroying it and that Hitler was his model when he was up on the stage and acting out his dream. When Moreno asked him what helped him to overcome his compulsion the man replied that he was surprised that besides himself there were so many people in the group who realized that they had a being like Adolf Hitler inside them and that had helped him.

The use of surplus reality is not only a clinical tool in treatment. It is a whole philosophical attitude towards life.

ZERKA: The real Adolf Hitler in Germany was to a degree lucky because he had auxiliary egos who believed in his cause and supported him.

Without his auxiliary egos he would have been unable to carry out his plans. The auxiliary egos were what kept him in power for as long as he was. Without auxiliary egos one cannot interact. We are not alone as actors on this earth. The stage in psychodrama gives protagonists the necessary auxiliary egos so they can start to relate and act. By these means we are warming them up to face the world outside. They are enabled to step out of their introversion and their fantasy world. Why did I accept this man with his fantasy children? Remember that I said the deepest catharsis in psychodrama comes from doing those scenes, those realities, those relationships, which may never happen, but which we need to happen. He needed that experience in order to be able to let go.

Chapter 8

Psychodrama as healing theatre

Therapeutes *were those in ancient Greece who were the disciples of the cult of Asclepius, the god of healing. His father, Apollo, the god of knowledge and consciousness, was also one of the gods who sent plagues and diseases down to earth. A disease was an expression of the wounded god. In Greek mythology many gods were wounded and suffered some incurable conditions. Dionysus, for instance, suffered from mania and Hercules suffered from epilepsy. These wounds and incurable conditions were inflicted upon man. The god was the sickness, but he was also the remedy and, therefore, the divine physician. What the therapist did was to create the* divina afflictio *which 'contains its own diagnosis, therapy, and prognosis, provided that the right attitude toward it is adopted' (Meier 1989: 3).*

In psychotherapy it is of great importance that we achieve the right attitude towards diseases. The symptoms of neurosis or depression, for example, can be seen not only as conditions one seeks to eliminate, but as an encounter with a specific perspective. These symptoms are entrances to certain tasks with which the patient has to learn to deal. The word 'patient' means suffering or endurance, but it also means to stay calm and wait, to be 'patient'. Pain, whatever it may be, has no place in our culture. It is only something to be eliminated, and we have no patience whatsoever to stand it for one minute more than we need to. But suffering is a means by which we can develop depth. Patience also means to stay open and not to interfere with the process.

Is it sometimes indicated that the right attitude for the therapist might be to support patience and the right attitude towards suffering in the patient? Suffering has always had a place in religions to purify the soul or to make the person find a deeper meaning in their condition. From this perspective a depression is not seen as something meaningless, but as a basis for creating meaning.

DAG: Zerka, do you agree that suffering can deepen a person?

ZERKA: With emotional suffering and pain, some people sink because they cannot bear it and others swim and come out well, deepened and developed in many ways. Therapists are supposed to relieve pain, not add to it. Furthermore, it has been found that people who were exposed to long endurance of severe physical pain as, for instance, patients with cancer, were at risk because their immune system ceased to function properly over time. So we have to make some distinctions. It is a very delicate subject. I do not have complete answers. Where do we go with pain? In psychotherapy and in psychodrama we can actually enter the pain, and this is done in psychic healing and in meditative healing as well. It is very much like a role reversal with the affliction. One is not asked to eliminate the pain, but asked to go into it and, by these means, it often disappears. There are different ways of dealing with pain which are more productive than either drugging it away or letting it just be. I do not see any purpose in people suffering for the sake of suffering if something can be done to enable them to suffer less. We are frequently learning that physicians do not study good pain management and thereby patients become debilitated, especially the elderly.

If I may refer to my own past severe pain in my shoulder due to a sarcoma, I experienced pain as a very isolating thing. One is totally absorbed, incarcerated and separated from the rest of the world. It is almost impossible at that stage to go beyond that level of pain and extend oneself.

The original power of healing was the encounter with Asclepius which took place at Epidaurus, his sanctuary. The patients who came there were introduced and initiated into the cult of the mystery of healing. The god was the physician, whose role in the mystery was to take on the disease of the patient as well as the quality of healing. He appeared in the dream of the patient who was lying on the klina, *the bed. And thus the healing process took place.*

Hippocrates, who introduced scientific medicine, regarded himself as a student of Asclepius. However, he instructed the client how to come to terms with his/her condition rather than letting the god do the whole process of healing. The disease was therefore separated from the physician. Thus, the physician, a human being, bestowed on himself a god-like quality, but he ascribed to himself only half the quality of the god, the aspect of healing, and rejected the dark side of healing, that is, the disease. This became the model for all physicians. When the psychotherapist does not take on the wound, thus splitting the original role of the healer/god, s/he gives him-/herself recognition for something which actually belongs to the god Asclepius: the mystery of healing. This form of self-deification may be abused. Many patients become victims of such power when human-being physicians are possessed by this god complex.

> *In der Wendung zum Besseren, bei einer schweren Krankheit des dem Tode ausgelieferten Lebewesen . . . bleibt immer etwas Unfaßbares, selbst wenn der Arzt die Ursache der Krankheit erkannt und entfernt hat. Denn es muß neben dem Einwirken des Arztes immer noch etwas mithelfen, das gleichzeitig mit dem Eingreifen von außen im Innern des Kranken vor sich geht, damit sich die Heilung einstellt. Im entscheidenden Moment der Heilwendung wirkt etwas, das am ehesten dem Ergießen einer Quelle zu vergleichen wäre.*[1]
>
> *(Kerényi 1948:32)*

For psychodramatists it could sometimes be beneficial to adopt the old concept of healing, to create the right attitude towards the psychodrama by remembering the mystery.

Psychodrama is not merely the representation of life and neither can a psychodrama alone change a person's life. However, psychodrama in itself is a real life experience and as such deepens the person. It puts him/her in contact with dimensions which belong more to religion than to concrete life situations. As such it can throw a light and a meaning on the life situation of the participant. Therefore, patience is a greater key to change than most psychodrama therapists realize.

DAG: I would like to go back to the roots and the idea of psychodrama as a healing theatre. The idea of theatre and healing goes back to ancient Greece and to the god Asclepius, son of Apollo.

ZERKA: Moreno did not see classical theatre as a healing theatre. He saw it as an aesthetic experience and I agree with him. Aristotle's idea of catharsis, which was one of the motivating forces of Moreno's thought, should be looked at as Moreno looked at it, from the spectator's point of view. Aristotle expected the spectator watching a tragedy to achieve a purging of two emotions mostly. Such a pair of emotions could be pity and fear, pity and terror or pity and awe. Maybe awe is the greatest emotion in that it can include the others.

Moreno focused first on the spectator. What is the spectators' experience? Are they really being purged or are they aware that these actors are not the real people? The actors do not cry real tears, they do not experience real joy. They are representations of the experience as written by a playwright. It is not their own direct human experience.

Then Moreno turned his eyes on the actors themselves and produced a theatre of healing by removing the script altogether and going back to the actors as real people, their pain, their laughter, their tears, their joy and anguish. Because people watching this know that the actor is a real person, they themselves are profoundly touched. They share a common humanity, and then they can even cry. Now that does not mean that people do not cry in a classical theatre when the production is particularly sad or beautiful, but they know it is not real. So from a secondary catharsis, as described by Aristotle, Moreno produced a primary action catharsis in the actor and a primary spectator catharsis in the group present. I do not like to use the word 'audience' any longer. This is not an audience, this is a group having a common experience.

DAG: Does Moreno want you to encounter the Godhead, the Creator, during the drama?

ZERKA: I assume he had that in mind when he spoke about children wanting to play 'God'. He saw them as wanting to be God. What they are really doing is re-empowering themselves. What we are doing in psychodrama is re-empowering the protagonist and the group members, and we are doing that because we are touching the autonomous healing centre. There are many people who do not become protagonists but heal by participating in other people's dramas as auxiliary egos or group members. Many times in sharing, people in the group will say 'Thank you so much' to the protagonist. 'You have done my psychodrama for me. You have given me insights that are absolutely priceless.' This aspect of sharing is a vitally healing phase of psychodrama.

DAG: The ancient Greeks believed that there were different gods for different life situations: gods for love, for epilepsy, for anger, for war, but also gods for diseases. It was the gods who made you sick, but they were also the cure. So the healing aspect was never human. The Greeks called a disease 'divine sickness'. In a way this thought is very creative. However, this archaic thinking can become very frightening in relation to diseases like AIDS. Can we really call a physical or emotional sickness something divine?

ZERKA: We do not really know how illness crosses the barrier from mind to body. We are now aware that the body remembers when the mind forgets. Even psychosomatic medicine only has some vague knowledge about the connection between body and mind. The medical model on one hand gives us a great deal of security. You go to a doctor and they seem to know what they are doing. On the other hand, there are a lot of illnesses that science cannot account for, as, for instance, in my own case.

There may be two people, same age, same disease and apparently with the same amount of vigour. One dies and the other survives. We have all heard that rather bitter pronouncement: 'The operation was successful but the patient died', which indicates that even doctors sometimes recognize healing as a mystery beyond human control.

Why do some people seem to get well when they go to Lourdes[2] for example? Millions of people go there. What is it that heals them? Is it their belief, their faith or the divinity of the Virgin Mary? I do think healing is a mystery.

DAG: Some people who have faced cancer or a similarly severe illness address this later as one of the best things that happened in their life. Do you see a relation to the idea of the 'divine sickness'?

ZERKA: I used to say about my sarcoma, 'I do not really recommend such a serious life-threatening illness for a Sunday afternoon picnic'. It is not that kind of joy. It is a very bitter journey, but all bitter journeys have two options: you either sink or swim. It is very much like fine steel which has to go through very hot fire. It cannot be made unless it is very hot. So it is like going through hot fire, like going through hell and coming out clearer, deeper, wiser, more compassionate and humane and, perhaps, even more spiritual.

One reaches for a divinity, whether it is within the self or some healing power outside the self. For me it was both a black and a white experience caused by the uncertainty as to whether I was really cured of my bone cancer with the amputation of my arm and shoulder.

I once described this experience as going through a very dark tunnel. At its end was a little light. If I could just reach the light I would be all right. When I came out into the light I knew, 'Hey, I really am going to be well. I am going to live. This is not going to catch me. It is not my time yet.' But now that I have been through that, how do I make the best of this new life I have been granted? In a sense, it is like being reborn.

Every profound personal experience is like a rebirth and lifts you to a different level of awareness. So from that point of view I can understand it when people say, 'It was the best thing that ever happened to me'. Even some of the people with HIV/ARC/AIDS say that. Some of them felt so much love and compassion from their community before they died that it gave their life an intensity it never had before.

I seriously believe that if we were to live forever, life would be miserable and perhaps even dreadful. Nothing in life really dies, things transmute. I am a profound believer in the transformation of souls. Our body is something that we just shed. It is really not that important. It is lent to us and we are responsible for taking care of it.

Far more important is what you do with your soul. How do you make it a refined instrument after you have gone through a purgatory like a critical illness?

I have seen many people come through that purgatory feeling elevated. But other people go under. I believe that we die when we have to die. Even people who commit suicide may have had to die at that time, in that way. Otherwise, they would have saved themselves. I believe that they will be reincarnated. It is generally considered among the people who have this idea about life and death, that those people who die most violently such as, for instance, in war or in the Holocaust, will reincarnate faster than anyone else, as if they are propelled by this tremendous energy of violence to turn it into something creative and positive again. There are some psychiatrists who are now finding younger people with memories of the Holocaust which would suggest that they are reincarnated Holocaust victims.

Sometimes we see people whose lives have already left them. That has nothing to do with age. You can see that even in a very young person. The creative spark is gone.

DAG: The therapist should assist the god of the healing cult. He is not the cause of the healing process. To what extent is a director such an assistant?

ZERKA: I regard myself as a channel. Very often insights come to me from God knows where. I say, 'from up above'. I do my best work when my ego is not in it. This is not something to satisfy my ego. By being an open channel, astounding information comes to me.

Let me tell you this story. I used to have these open sessions in Beacon, New York. Once I had 35 people from a graduate school whom I had not met before. Since they were unfamiliar with psychodrama I started a lecture to warm them up. When I finished a sentence, all of a sudden I had the feeling of floating two or three inches above the stage and a hand was gently but very directly pushing me over to a young woman sitting in the front row. For a moment I asked myself, 'What am I doing?' An inner voice said, 'No, no, do not ask, just go'. I had no idea what was going to happen. But I went up to her and said, 'Give me the pills. I know you're planning to commit suicide with them'. She opened her handbag and out came a vial of pills. Everyone in the room was absolutely breathless. They must have thought, 'This woman is some kind of a witch'. So I told one of my students, 'You know where the bathroom is. Take Mary to the bathroom and be sure she flushes all those pills down the toilet. When you come back, we'll work on what is causing this, and what is the reason for this desire to kill yourself.' When the two returned, the psychodrama began.

The opening interview revealed that three weeks earlier, her fiancé, whom she was due to marry at the end of the semester, had been killed in a motorcar accident whilst under the influence of LSD. They found this out when they did the autopsy. After his funeral his parents developed a *folie à deux*, 'He is not dead, he is just away, he is going to come back'. Whenever she goes to see them, because she needs to mourn him and talk about him, they say, 'How dare you talk like that? You are a wicked girl, he is not dead, he's coming home soon.' 'So', Mary said, 'I am going crazy.'

I immediately reproduced the accident with her in the role of her fiancé. I had chairs placed on the stage, suggested she sit as if in a car, and asked some men to come up and push her off the stage. She fell, and was lying on the ground, below the stage. I went up to her and said: 'George, you know what happened to you? You can talk now, because in psychodrama everyone can speak when they want or need to. Can you hear me?' 'Yes.' 'Do you know what Mary is planning to do? Would you pick someone here to be Mary?' He/she picked a little girl. By this time, nearly everybody was crying.

Little Mary came up and she cried too. She understood exactly what she had to do without any prompting. She grabbed hold of the protagonist and said, 'George, I have got to die. I have got to be with you. I do not want to be separated from you. Your parents won't admit that you're dead. I am going absolutely mad.' The protagonist sat up straight, took on a very strong voice, put his arm around her and said, 'No. You must not do this. It was an accident. Nobody told me I should not have driven the car under the influence of LSD. I did not know better. But you will only make me feel worse if you join me. I am so sorry to have left you. We had planned a good life together. I want you to go on living. Never mind my parents. They are not your problem. They will have to make their peace with this in their own way. Your problem is for you to live. That is what I want for you. Your dying would only add to my guilt. I want you to live your life to the full.' We did the role reversal so Mary could hear George's message. That was the entire psychodrama. Of course there was a lot of sharing afterwards, and ideas of suicide were spoken about and what these experiences mean to us. Here you see the divine madness. On one hand the man had killed himself by accident. She thought he wanted to pull her over to his side through suicide, to death. On the other hand in the psychodrama he became her therapist who regarded his intoxicated driving as wrong-doing and assured her that her life must be lived.

DAG: In central European folklore evil can grow out of dead people. The souls of murdered people, of people who died violently, through suicide or in a battle, i.e., people who died before their time and whose lives did not meet a natural end, out of their frustration turn into ghosts or demons. The ghost can only find peace by dragging somebody else over to the other side, to death. This can go on for generations where one suicide triggers off the next. Suicide is infectious, like an epidemic.

ZERKA: Sociometry teaches us that: 'We not only affect one another, we infect one another'. So here you see a very profound infection. It can be emotional, it can be physical, and it can be both. The ancient idea of the divine madness may very well be active in sociometry and treatable by psychodrama.

DAG: You mentioned earlier that it is so important to be open and to function as a channel. Moreno stated that the director should be a catalyst for the drama and the group which, of course, included the spiritual dimension. On the contrary, many students in the dogmatic and immovable countries of Europe are nowadays trained in a concept called *Der rote Faden* (The Red Thread). The 'red thread' is a concept in which directors or students are encouraged to immediately diagnose and to quickly establish a plan as to where the session should go. The work is very structured and you must know what you are doing and why. In short, the director knows everything about the problem, its cause and effect, its cure, and the protagonist knows nothing. The 'red thread' is for the director and not for the protagonist. The directors are not assisting any more, they have taken over the sessions. Do you think that is correct?

ZERKA: When I direct a session I am a blank slate, a blank screen. Most of the time I do not have any preconceived notions. Psychodrama is first of all an experience. I want to experience whatever the protagonists are experiencing. However, sometimes protagonists have a specific problem they need to work on. I allow myself to be guided by them but I try not to be too fixed at the start.

Get away from your preconceived notions. Listen with the heart, not just with the mind. Let it reverberate in you. At times something goes 'ping, ping' in me. It is what Moreno called 'tele' or 'medial understanding'. If you are open to it, it comes. You can have a red thread and it can be very useful, but you can find it is the wrong thread. There may be other red threads, which are thicker, heavier, deeper and darker.

DAG: The 'red thread' is something that comes to you, not something that you create.

ZERKA: You do not impose it. It emerges from the protagonist.

DAG: Or maybe from the drama?

ZERKA: From the drama also. Actually it arises from the interaction between the director and the protagonist, and the protagonist and the auxiliaries. However, you do not always know it. I teach my students to be naive, they should not know so much. Even if you have worked with this person before, three weeks ago, s/he may not be the same person. S/he may have gone through a series of experiences which may have changed him/her. Be open to change! Do not always harken back to what they were three weeks ago, unless it is something threatening of which you need to make them aware. The protagonist may be different from before. Spontaneity changes us. Moreno's position was that the director has to be the most spontaneous member of the group. How can one be spontaneous if a fixed notion takes precedence?

DAG: Could you tell me something about your thoughts regarding transference in relationship to tele?

ZERKA: When I have worked with people in a group and then have them in personal sessions, I did not like working with them as well as working in the group because the transference can get very murky. Projection is never a healthy thing. When someone projects upon me, I am aware that they do not really see me. Transference clasps a mask over my face. They are putting their needs and their helplessness on me.

DAG: This sort of transference the client can put upon the director or therapist can be very dangerous, because the therapist or the director could now think they are the healer. The healing process is no longer in the hands of the gods, but in the hands of human beings.

Hippocrates made the following separation which did not exist before. Let me quote C.A. Meier for you:

> The inner connection between the divine sickness and the divine physician formed the core of the art of healing in the ancient world. But ancient Greek scientific medicine was developed along with theurgic medicine. It was developed to combat disease. The disease was now separate from the physician himself . . . This attribution of divine quality to the physician is not without its dangers, for it exposes him to the risk of inflation.
>
> (Meier 1989: 7–8)

Do you not think there is a risk that directors of psychodrama take on themselves this divine healing power and become inflated?

ZERKA: I think this happens when they lose contact with the protagonist. They do not produce good psychodramas. It is very frustrating and irritating to watch that. I do not let that happen any more. When I see it happening to students I pull them up sharply, and I say, 'You are not listening. I do not know what you are doing, but you are not listening. Let us go back and listen to what the protagonist has just produced and let us see what you have seen. What have you heard? Why are you superimposing your own ideas on this, because I do not think you are with it.' It is destructive to the psychotherapeutic process because you lose your protagonist. You are not dealing with him/her on a level on which the protagonist needs to be dealt with. The translation of 'therapist' is 'servant'. So we are the servants in the healing process.

Chapter 9

Psychodrama as tragedy

Aristotle thought it was tragedy's main purpose and power to make the spectator and the audience believe that such persons as they saw on stage could really act and talk the way they did. A tragedy could, therefore, only have an effect if the audience accepted it and if, in Morenian terms, they could make a role reversal with the persons on stage. The staged tragedy was thus paralleled in ordinary life: both the theatrical production and quotidian life are linked by what Aristotle called 'universal'.

Attic tragedies were written to be performed only once in the tragic festivals. Sometimes these tragedies were new, but usually an old one was rewritten or parts from old tragedies were put into a new context. Hence a tragedy reflected the Zeitgeist (the Spirit of the Time); it showed the shifts in the current rhetoric of Athens and the audience could also perceive its shifting conditions. So the spectators very often came to see how the old stories would be told this year.

In the tragic theatre the audience learned that the world is not the way we like it to be and that our capability of acting freely is limited by preconditions. Tragedy is the representation of an archetypal world through which it mirrors reality with understanding and compassion; it is thus an enemy of self-indulgent fantasy.

It is not moralizing in terms of telling right from wrong, but it reveals the conditions under which certain actions and their effects take place.

DAG: The word 'drama' means acting; the German word for it is *Handlung*. The drama was a structured dialogue between the leader of the chorus and the chorus. Before the development of the drama there was the tragedy, *tragoidia* in Greek, which literally means the 'goat-song'. The goat is a very sexually potent animal. It also represented the god Dionysus in mythology. The 'goat-song' was a mourning song for the death of the god Dionysus who was murdered several times but always returned. Therefore, he is the god of destruction *and* creativity. The goat-song or the mourning song was sung and acted in a state of ecstasy and it was totally unstructured. I, therefore, assume that mourning is one of the deepest feelings a human being can experience. It is deeper than anger, love or anything else and it is truly cathartic. I have come to the conclusion that directing a psychodrama is like directing a psycho-tragoidia.

ZERKA: People have to go through a mourning process when they have suffered a profound loss. They may accuse God for the deprivation. It is also an accusation directed at life, so to speak. They have to go through this loss. It is true. I had to mourn the loss of my limb, and that was part of my healing process. It is difficult to justify why a young woman of 40 should have a thing like this happen. When one gets a bad diagnosis, the first thing everybody thinks is, 'Why me? What have I done to deserve it? Is this a quid pro quo thing? Is this something that I owe somebody?'

DAG: Did you get an answer to these questions?

ZERKA: The answer is, 'This way lies madness'. There are no answers. It is a mystery. I asked my doctor, 'How did it happen?', and he said, 'Well, radiation in the air. Milk products. Cows pick up radiation in their food. We do not really know.' It is not genetic. No one in my family had anything like it. It is a rare condition, a cancer of the cartilage of the bone. So I realized that there are certain things for which there are no answers. Some things in life are mysteries. In fact, as I get older I have more and more respect for the mystery of life.

DAG: Can you describe your process of mourning?

ZERKA: For a long time I was extremely depressed. It disillusioned me that something like this could ever happen to me. I do not smoke, I do not drink, *why* did this happen? I had a small child to care for. How could I be so irresponsible as to die and leave a small child whose father is already in his late sixties? It is irresponsible. So I accused myself as well. There is much accusation going on in mourning. We go through hell accusing ourselves. That was all part of my mourning.

Then I realized that all this did not mean anything in the long run; there were no easy answers. The only answer was to live. Not many people come out of Memorial Hospital in New York City (the foremost hospital for cancer and allied diseases) with an assurance that they would live. It was not a profound assurance that I was given, but still it was enough to make me feel, 'Yes, I am going to manage. I am going to survive this.' I was fortunate. Before the amputation six doctors misdiagnosed me. I had walked around with a growing lump for fifteen months. It could have been too late already, but it was not. So, on the one hand, I thought 'I am a walking medical miracle'. On the other hand, I thought, 'Well, I was protected. I did not protect myself. Something divine, perhaps. My work was not finished yet.' Mourning is a very complex set of emotions.

DAG: In many places in the world there are professional wailers or, as they say in German, *Klageweiber*. These are usually elderly women who are paid to burst into tears, cry loudly while beating their chests and pulling out their hair as a means to trigger the bereaved's tears, lamenting and mourning.

ZERKA: That is a ritual, it can be a profound one and some people need it. It has a psychodramatic aspect. These women act as the Greek chorus and as auxiliary egos to help the warm-up of the mourners.

DAG: Maybe mourning in psychodrama or psycho-tragedy can also be a healing ritual because it is done in a group and not alone.

ZERKA: Absolutely. We mourn together. We mourn the loss and the suffering and the agony. When we do not mourn with the protagonist, the protagonist may feel abused. I have had a couple of sessions where it was very difficult for the group to mourn with the protagonist because he was so difficult and so unsympathetic as a personality. If the director is not able to produce that mourning in the group, the protagonist is left more alone than ever and has the feeling that he was not treated properly by the group. This is particularly true when the protagonist exhibits psychopathic behaviour. Then the group, representing public opinion, becomes the teacher to the protagonist by confronting that person with what may be immoral behaviour. In fact, under those conditions, the protagonist learns that his/her behaviour is unacceptable.

DAG: So maybe the mourning is a transpersonal experience between the group members.

ZERKA: I just remembered some words of St Augustine. 'The hearer [of the drama] is not expected to relieve, but merely invited to grieve.' Psychodrama is not just the theatre of grieving, but also of relieving. That is the major difference between legitimate drama and psychodrama. According to Daniel Boorstin in his book *The Creators*, what happened when the Dionysian festivals were transformed into Greek theatre was that the condition of the people present was changed. The festivals took place in the streets and everyone was involved in the action. The theatre was an artificial setting where 'citizens became witnesses' (Boorstin 1993: 207).

Chapter 10

Diagnosis in psychodrama

In psychiatry and psychotherapy there is a great deal of focus on finding a diagnosis, such as schizophrenia, which labels the patient. The word 'diagnosis' is of Greek origin. Gnosis means 'knowledge, cognition and cognizance'. Agnosis is the opposite. The word 'diagnosis' can be split up two ways: dia-gnosis and di-agnosis. The first version would, therefore, mean 'knowledge through cognizance'. The latter could be understood as 'taking away the not knowing'.

The word 'diagnosis' in psychiatry loses its impact: it should describe a process rather than an end product. What most professionals regard as a diagnosis is actually nothing more than categorization. The word 'category' also derives from ancient Greek. In its root it means to speak publicly in the marketplace. Categorization could then, if one so wishes, be understood as marketing a product, which to some extent patients are considered to be today.

DAG: Psychodrama is a method of clarification and action. In the roles we play in life we have a lot in common with other people, but we are also unique. Awareness of this differentiation and what one's unique place in this world looks like is vital. To find your own uniqueness in psychodrama in relation to the world is one of psychodrama's goals. It seems to me that you and J.L. Moreno were excellent diagnosticians. You put people in a process, you did not label them. You gave them an auxiliary world to relate to, for instance, in your treatment of hallucinations.

ZERKA: Moreno comes from a model of health, not from a model of pathology. He did not believe in labels. Unlike Freud he did not conceive the psyche as consisting of a number of layers. He did not think in those terms. He saw you in your totality and with your potential, not just with your failure. That was the difference. He would say even about a psychotic, 'Yes, the patient may be considered as displaying pathological spontaneity, but it is my task to turn it integrative rather than disintegrative'. He did not believe that if you have a category, if you name it, then you know it. He was not a linguist in that sense. The linguists believe you give it a label and then you know it. Nonsense. He did not believe that language is the royal route to or could absorb the entire psyche. Language does not convey everything you need to know.

For example we label foods. You go to the grocery store and you buy a jar of raspberry jam because you love that jam. You already have the experience of what raspberry jam tastes like and you know that you like the taste. But until you open *that* particular jar you do not know what *that* jam tastes like. It is exactly the same with people. You see certain patterns, you see certain phenomena. Let that particular person open up to you and you see something very different.

While Moreno did not use psychiatric diagnostic categorizations in his writing or teaching, as director of a psychiatric hospital it is clear that these categories were documented. Moreno would have lost his licence to run a mental hospital if he had not conformed. He was an excellent diagnostician in both senses of the word. When he labelled a patient with a psychiatric diagnosis he was generally right. In addition, he was true to the original meaning of the word 'diagnosis': 'to take away the not knowing'.

When my sister became his patient, for instance, he said to me: 'She has an excited depression'. This was in 1941, well before the term 'bi-polar' became the norm and of course, he referred to manic-depression of a specific kind.

When he was criticized for not communicating with his peers in the acceptable manner, he explained that diagnosis in psychodrama is very clearly illuminated by the process itself. Therefore, the director makes therapeutic and dramatic decisions based on the findings as the psychodrama proceeds. The diagnosis is made spontaneously and used to decide upon scenes and interactions. Our interpretation is tested out though not necessarily indicated to the protagonist or the group present, but instead put into immediate action. As students mature in the work, they become quite sophisticated in their grasp of what the director has constructed in the way of a diagnosis and they can see how that construct influences the drama as it unfolds.

Chapter 11

Sharing in psychodrama

Sharing is the last phase of a psychodrama; in it the group members share their feelings and experiences from their own lives as they refer to the psychodrama. One reason for the sharing phase is that the protagonist has revealed a great deal from his/her life and now should be getting something back from the group. This phase has a cathartic effect on the group members, who are able to relieve some tensions, which during the course of the drama have been building up. The following conversation may throw some other lights on sharing and to what extent the sharing should be protagonist-centred or directed to the drama's content.

DAG: Could you tell me about the history of sharing in psychodrama?

ZERKA: Occasionally we would bring patients from Beacon to the open sessions in New York City, which Moreno gave for mental health professionals. Instead of bringing the professionals up to Beacon, we took patients down to the city to demonstrate our work. Once in the late 40s Moreno brought a lovely young woman who became our protagonist. After the session the psychiatrists began to analyse and to interpret her. After the second or the third remark he saw that the girl was crumbling. She had come away from the session with a clear eye and a good feeling about herself, and now they were cutting her to pieces. They were disillusioning her.

Finally Moreno said, 'Stop. This is not good; not good for the protagonist, not really a good process. I will tell you why. All of you have different orientations and all of you will give a different interpretation. Now it is true that the patient has never had the attention of so many psychiatrists. That in itself is something worthwhile, it may make her feel better. However, that is not really what we want. We do not want you to be psychiatrists, we want you to be group members. We would like you to share from your own life.' Can you imagine psychiatrists talking about their own lives? It was a profound revolution. They are trained to maintain professional distance, or, as in psychoanalysis, to be a blank screen. So this idea of sharing of their private lives was quite a threat and completely out of their realm. It may well be that this was another reason why Moreno was so often met with hostility from the psychiatric fraternity.

DAG: Did this come as an impulse to J.L. Moreno at that moment?

ZERKA: As an awareness that this was not good processing for the protagonist. It was not useful as a psychodramatic entry into the group. He was not getting to the group. They were responding from the top of the head to the eyebrows, but not from the heart. Moreno explained, 'You know, when a person is a protagonist and denudes himself or herself in front of us, that is giving us a form of love. The only way to repay love is with love.'

DAG: What did you do before that?

ZERKA: Some directors like to interpret or give advice. In training we now teach them: 'Do not offer advice, be a human guide'. To the group members we say the same thing: 'Talk about yourself, please. Do not analyse or advise.' They have to be taught to have an open heart, not just a head.

So when the next person began to talk again in this rather haughty fashion, Moreno asked, 'Tell me, are you married? Do you have children? Is your daughter this age?' It turned out, as so often happens in psychodrama, that he had a daughter the same age as the protagonist with whom he was having a problem. 'That is what we need to talk about. Tell the protagonist in what way her drama touches upon your own life and experience with your daughter. Here you are a father. Never mind about your skills as a psychiatrist. That does not work here. We all have human problems.'

In fact, I had a classic example of that later on in the 50s. A psychiatrist came to Beacon as a patient and I had brought to Beacon a very disturbed young woman. She watched his session and came to me and said, 'That was the most important session I have attended yet, more important than my own. To see this gorgeous hunk of man, beautiful, handsome, well put together, falling apart in front of my eyes and having exactly the same problem in his marriage that I am having, that was really a lesson for me.' So here we see the reverse: the revealing of self as a human being who has also failed or is also failing.

DAG: This was also what the patient in the psychodrama of Adolf Hitler said: that it helped him to see so many other patients discovering the Hitler within themselves.

However, the following story brought me into a dilemma concerning sharing. I had to make a decision whether the sharing is for the protagonist or for the psychodramatic production by the group. Because, if it is the latter it has many more perspectives than only the protagonist's. The following situation happened to me. I had a man in a group. His concern was that he had killed a boy through drunken driving. He was in great grief and could not imagine how his life could go on even though he served a two-year sentence. I had no idea that there was a woman in the group who had lost her child to a drunk driver. Her sharing was not very supportive to the protagonist. In fact, she said that people like him had no right to live. What do you think?

ZERKA: It was right that she was allowed to share from her point of view and her pain. It may even have been good for him, because he had all that guilt anyway. Here was the accusation, which he deserved and asked for. Maybe he was also asking to be punished, and he got it. But in addition they could have role-reversed.

Let me tell you another story. A young man came to our bi-weekly sessions in New York and wanted to be part of a therapy group. He was Catholic, his older brother was a priest, and he had just discovered that he himself was gay. Everybody in the group accepted it. There was no harshness or judgement. He went away and later called me on the phone to say, 'I cannot join your group'. I asked, 'Why not?'. 'Because you all accept me.' I replied, 'You do not accept your self'. 'No, I need punishment.' He needed to be the Catholic priest his brother was who told him he was going to go to hell. I had not explored his need for punishment because we have always been taught to be supportive. Being supportive in this case meant giving him the punishment he required to cleanse himself.

DAG: Sharing is very important because it diminishes the transference in the group.

ZERKA: Right. Sharing is the group-psychotherapeutic aspect of psychodrama, besides participating as auxiliary ego on the stage. It is the place where group psychodrama becomes group psychotherapy.

Chapter 12

The creation of the double

The double technique, together with the mirror technique and role reversal, is a major psychodramatic technique. J.L. Moreno, conducting a public session, presented the subject of the double as follows:

> *What do you see on a psychodrama stage? You may, for example, see a certain person who is a mental patient. This person is mentally in such a condition that communication is extremely difficult. A nurse cannot talk to her, a doctor cannot relate to her. Then you use psychodrama in the following way: You take this patient, let's call her Mary, and you say to her, Now, you may have lost any kind of contact with your father, with your mother, with your sister, with your brother. You may have lost contact with your husband, or your fellow human beings, but if you could only talk to yourself. If you could only talk to that person who is closest to you, with whom you are best acquainted. If we could produce for you the double of yourself, then you would have somebody with whom you could speak, with whom you could act together, because you belong together.*
>
> *(J.L. Moreno 1987: 129–130)*

J.L. Moreno relates the development of the double technique, as he did with the other major psychodramatic techniques, to the developmental stages of a child. After a child is born it goes through a few weeks of a very particular existence, which he calls 'the matrix of identity'. In this phase the child lives in a state in which the mother, other persons, the infant him- or herself, and all objects belong to a single universe – a single whole. There is no differentiation yet between an inner and an outer world.

However, it is then and there that for all movements, perceptions, actions and interactions, the phenomenon of the double is activated for the first time. You may say that it is there that an experiment of nature is in progress, which I have called the 'double'. Whatever happens later on during the growth of that infant, this primary conflict foreshadows its destiny. It emerges from it, grows and differentiates further, and develops.

When a protagonist has a double on stage that really touches his/her soul their relation resembles this matrix of identity. When they are on this level they are almost like one person. However, the process which takes place between them is not only empathy. Moreno regarded empathy as a one-way process. He believed there is a process taking place in both persons which goes beyond a mutual empathy. He called this process in which thoughts and feelings of both participants interweave 'two-way empathy'. Both enter each other's mind and influence one another. This phenomenon is the process that J.L. Moreno called 'tele'.

DAG: Regarding the idea of the double or the *Doppelgänger*, do you think there is another Zerka Moreno walking around on this earth?

ZERKA: I would love to meet her. It would be a little scary, however. Why would I love to meet her? I might learn something from her and I might be able to teach her something, too. It would be instructive. You know, when I was a youngster, I used to rush around corners wondering if there was a double who would meet me. My mother had bought me a dirndl dress[1] in Germany and I once wore it when I went to school. Another girl met me also dressed in a dirndl which was different from mine. Hers was the Austrian kind with the black background; mine was brown with brown flowers. We looked at each other and were absolutely astonished. I had never seen anybody with a dirndl dress before. It was a little bit like meeting your double, but not quite.

When as a child I used to rush around corners to try and find my double, it might have been related to that shadow or imaginary companion that children often produce.

DAG: Did your companion in Holland look and talk like you?

ZERKA: No, we did not talk to each other. We were too shy. We were about 7 years old. She did not look like me, really. But she was a cute little girl. We made a little dance in front of each other not knowing whether to go left or right until she motioned, 'You go this way and I'll go that way'. Then we looked back and waved at each other. I never saw her again. I realized that it was not a true double because it was only partial, even the clothes were not the same. However, externals never fooled me. Even as a child I must have been quite wise. I could see people who were ugly, but had beautiful souls and people who were beautiful, but had terrible souls. So the externals did not bother me too much.

DAG: When did Moreno come up with the idea of the double?

ZERKA: That may have been when he was lonely. As he explained to the patient, Mary: 'When you are lonely and you have no one to talk to, who do you talk to but yourself? You reflect with yourself about the self.'

The idea of the double actually is an old mythological notion. Moreno thought that maybe God produced us all twice. One of us is kept with God and the other is sent down to the world. That is the reason why he/she knows everything about us. Because our double up there reflects everything we are doing. That connects to how parents punish naughty children, telling them: 'God sees everything you do', which implies something negative, a punishment in the hereafter. Moreno turned that idea into a positive and integrative technique as well as a romantic notion in life. I think his is a wonderful idea. When you die, you are reunited with your double without punishment and thus strengthened. Nobody else has ever had that idea. I think it is beautiful.

When Moreno worked with patients he often had a practical problem. They could not account for why they were sick, or they were not used to talking to a therapist. So he would say, 'Do you talk to yourself?' and fortunately they often responded 'Yes'. 'Well, this is just like talking to yourself. I'll just give you somebody else to stand next to you to be that part of you that talks to itself.'

DAG: Do you agree that the double brings another you to the surface?

ZERKA: Many parts of you. The idea that a human being is an individual, not further divisible, is of course a mistake; we are many, many parts, roles and beings. The word 'individual' is misleading.

You know something about what has been going on inside you, or you arouse that awareness in the protagonist. As a double, for example, you might say: 'Was I always this unhappy? I do not think I can remember a time when I was happy. Let's look at that for a minute.' Challenging and arousing.

I think there are two reasons why J.L. used a double a lot more than I do. One is that we had these very bizarre patients; if not frankly psychotic they were very much on the edge. These patients could not be understood except in terms of their own rationale, and the best way to get at that was to have a double who is able to tap into that. The double is a real bridge between the protagonist and the director.

The other reason is the following: when he was conducting training sessions for professional groups he was teaching them in the open session how to get inside the psyche of the protagonist. You do not have to do that alone as a director, you use a member of your team. In psychodrama we work as a team. Moreno was the first psychiatrist to bring teamwork into psychiatry.

So what became operationally effective was also to display (because this person was very much on display in a teaching session) the inside of that person. I use the double less and less these days. I turn the protagonists into their own doubles.

In my training with Moreno the instructions he gave the auxiliary ego double was that the protagonist represented the outside, unable to express the inside. The task of the auxiliary was to represent the protagonist's inside. I turn that around and say to the protagonist: 'Well, we have seen some of the outside of you. Let somebody be the outside of you, and you be your own inside, your own double.' That works very well.

DAG: I, as your trainee, have heard you talk several times about your sister Binky, and how important she has been in your life because she confronted you with craziness and it was her illness that brought you two to Moreno. Were you her double?

ZERKA: It is possible that I did not know what it was, but that I really became her double at some point, because then I knew there was something seriously wrong with her. But I could never talk about it to anyone. I was about 8 years old. If I had gone and told our mother that there was something wrong with my sister, she would have said: 'You are a wicked child. You must not talk like that about your sister, she is so good, so angelic. Do not come and tell me bad things about your good sister. You are the naughty one, the bad girl! Go to your room! I do not want to see you.' So I kept it to myself.

My sister and I used to do exercises when we were young, lying in bed at night, to see if we could transmit images to each other. She was good at sending them, I was much better at receiving them. When I tried sending them to her she did not receive them. So you have hit on something rather important that never occurred to me, that I probably did a lot of doubling. I was about 10 or 11 years old at that point. In fact, the images she sent were like in a movie. I would say, 'I see a train coming', and she would reply, 'That's right'. The image was that of a train running overhead.

DAG: You said that your sister could send images, but she could not receive them.

ZERKA: Maybe from other people, but not from me. She was not so good at that.

DAG: Do you think she could double you?

ZERKA: No. She was me once in role reversal, when I had shown her how I felt. But I do not think she could really double me, I doubt that she really knows who I am. I intimidate her, she respects me, and in some ways she is in awe of me. But I do not think she could double me, she is not integrated enough. You have to be quite well-integrated to be able to do that with another person. She is not that well-integrated; not in this lifetime, maybe in another lifetime. She could be very motherly when I was small, loving and very caring, and it was wonderful when she began to have a bosom. I liked to rest in bed close to her. My mother was not often available and so it was nice to have an older sister like that. So in some ways she was a protective figure, but also at times a threatening one. My sense is that she did not know she was threatening.

DAG: The doubling experience is a very profound one. But I have seen that it often happens that self-declared doubles step upon the stage to throw in a sentence to present an insight or an opinion; or the double is used to steer the psychodrama in a certain direction.

ZERKA: I think it is an imposition and can be manipulative. I ask the protagonist, 'Do you want a double?' I believe students and directors sometimes want to show how clever they are, or they are overheated. Sometimes a group member wants to be up there as the protagonist or competes with the director and wants to take over the session. Therefore, it is important that the protagonist accepts the double. So I might ask the protagonist, 'Is that right, is the double correct?' That empowers rather than undermines the protagonist.

When working with patients the use of doubles is very productive, because you learn things about the patient that might otherwise not come to light so readily. They may not tell you some things, but they might tell their double. One of the rules is: 'Do not overwhelm or take over for the protagonist'. In the beginning, when we first started learning to double we often overwhelmed the protagonist with our awareness and that was not always helpful; the protagonist may not be ready for such insight.

The double has to feel into the protagonist, to get the images and also the moods, colours and rhythm of that protagonist. Afterwards doubles can take over their protagonist's headache or stomach ache; they can feel them. Then auxiliaries have to shake off the identity of the protagonist. This is not only true of the double function but also of taking a difficult role of a significant absent other related to the protagonist. Sometimes I suggest to an auxiliary or a double, 'Do you need to get free of the role? Move about, shake, and get rid of the role any way you need to.' One can really take over other people's ills this way if one is sensitive or especially vulnerable and does not know how to protect the self. We do that with any troubling role and call it 'de-roling'.

DAG: So, in a way, you are still using the double in that even though you do not always pick the person from the group, you let the person double him-/herself?

ZERKA: I may ask, 'Is this a scene in which you need a double? Do you need a double right now?' Then the protagonists can decide for themselves. Moreno used to assign us the task of the auxiliary or double because his psychotic patients would not have known whom to pick anyway. We worked very intensely with psychotic patients until we got them clear. Moreno thought that he knew which auxiliary to pick because he knew some of our role repertoire or he trusted our intuition. Besides, there was in the beginning no model for this work, we built it as we went along. When we began to work with the normal or near normal we allowed them to pick their own auxiliaries. This also gave us insight into the sociometric structure of the group.

DAG: Personally I do not use doubles in the training as much as I did earlier. I tend to have a dialogue with inner and outer figures.

ZERKA: So do I, but doubling can be a productive technique. One wonderful aspect of psychodrama is its flexibility. As a subjective–objective actor one can go back and forth, because one is actually close to being another person. One takes a privileged walk in the psyche of another person.

Chapter 13

Projection and participation mystique in psychodrama

Many psychodramatists have raised the question: what did Moreno mean by the term 'object tele'? There is a common misunderstanding among many that tele only relates to other human beings, that it means to look upon oneself with the others' eyes. Tele encompasses animals, gods, matter, in short, every imaginable being or object. It is true that an animal, for example, cannot make a complete role reversal with us but we are able to role-reverse with the animal. Tele is an inter-phenomenon. The prefix 'inter' here means 'between'. Literally translated from Greek, 'tele' refers to distance, be it between two or more. From a Morenian perspective tele could be defined as 'the between distance', all of the energies flowing in the distance between two or more. It is never an intra-phenomenon even if we are discussing auto-tele, which refers to the different relationships within one's own role repertoire.

The concept of tele, which at the core is a sociometric concept, is essentially energy moving 'between' and relates to spontaneity, creativity and action. Tele is, therefore, always active, never passive. This energy also involves the imaginal dimension. One produces images of a person one is about to meet, or what will happen the next evening with one's lover, for example. Tele as an inter-phenomenon relates to individuals, dyads, groups and the cosmos. It stretches far beyond our usual definition of objective and subjective reality where we believe that objective reality is social, commonly shared and physical, whereas subjective reality deals with individual psychological reality. In psychological reality we include fantasy, images, wishes, dreams and exclude everything that belongs to so-called objective reality. This psychological reality is not physical, not commonly shared and not social. The word 'real' does not give us much information as to what something is, but rather tells us what something is not. For many people psychological reality is 'not' real.

The French Dadaist and poet Pierre Reverdy who was well acquainted with Tristan Tzara and the Dadaist circle in Zurich wrote a statement in 1918 which later became one of the foundations of the surrealist movement and relates very well to psychodrama and surplus reality:

> *The image is a pure creation of the mind. It cannot be born of a comparison but from a juxtaposition of two more or less distant realities. The more the relationship between the two juxtaposed realities is distant and true, the stronger the image will be – the greater is its emotional power and poetic reality.*
>
> *(Reverdy, quoted in Breton 1972: 20)*

This chapter draws attention to the fact that such a division between physical and psychological reality is of no importance and that is true in the psychodramatic realm, where the separation between psyche and matter does not exist. Zerka Moreno believes that tele is love, liking and respect at the same time. Since tele involves this kind of attraction and respect it has the same qualities as seen in the Greek goddess Aphrodite, who was the goddess of beauty, love and fertility and required respect. Lack of respect for her also meant lack of respect for the world, as she represented the soul of the world in the 'appearance' of all mundane matter – trees, wells, and everything else. Tele is a process of the soul, since it connects people to the meaning of love and beauty, as reflected in one another, the world, and the gods.

Western societies pay much attention to the differentiation between subjective and objective reality. An inability to distinguish between the inner imaginal world and the outer reality-oriented world is seen as a disturbance. Psychologists refer to this lack of distinction as the 'projection phenomenon', whereas anthropologists such as Levy-Brühl address this archaic identification as 'participation mystique'. He defines participation mystique as:

> *a form of relationship with an object (meaning thing) in which the subject cannot distinguish himself from the thing. This rests on the notion, which may be prevalent in a culture that the person/tribe and the thing – for instance a cult object or holy artefact – are already connected. When the state of participation mystique is entered, this connection comes to life.*
>
> *(Plaut 1986)*

Do we really wish to believe in a world without soul and without gods? Do we want to believe in a world in which only human beings are equipped with soul, as is commonly assumed? Should prayers to the Virgin Mary mean only that believers pray to a statue? Should the holy cows in Hinduism be seen as a symptom of psychopathology and primal disturbances? Is religion as seen in modern psychotherapy only a sign of pathology?

Dividing reality into subjective and objective creates several similarities with the psychopathic relation to the world. The psychopathic personality tends to live in a world of 'materia' that has no soul. This kind of encounter with the world is unfortunately becoming commonplace – everything and everyone being only dead matter. We use and are used. There is no respect save for one's own self and needs.

On the psychodrama stage we, on the contrary, engage in 'participation mystique'. There everything has soul and spirit. In Judaeo-Christian tradition, when God created man from clay his 'spiritus' turned lifeless matter into life. On the magical psychodrama stage we do not separate realities. Psyche and materia are the same thing – everything comes alive.

DAG: In psychotherapy the concept of projection means that one is placing an inner content onto an outer object in space. The borders between the inner and the outer world are therefore significant when working with projections. The psychodrama stage, our main tool, was designed in the form of a circle, contained within itself. It has no beginning and no end. On the stage surplus reality is of the essence and comes into existence. We as psychodramatists need to follow the protagonist's perception of the world. How valid is it, then, to work with projection in psychodrama?

ZERKA: Let us look at the people who come to us with their concerns. Protagonists, whether patients, clients or other persons, are encouraged to explore their lives in action. They come to us with their problems, pains and perceptions, whatever they are. The only way to change people is through relationships. We are relationship therapists. Relationships include relations with people who may be absent or present, animals, objects, values, the deceased, or possibly God.

From a materialistic point of view, nobody can totally take the part of another human being. You cannot really exchange bodies, but psychodramatically you can approximate certain feelings of the other, in the role of the other. What occurs in role reversal is that your perception in the role of the other begins to change when you shut off your own person. In taking the role of the other you can come very close to the essence of that person by looking upon the world through his/her eyes. That also includes experiencing their sociometric relations, their feelings, their body perception. This role reversal on stage is a transformational process into the other person. In a materialistic sense, role reversal is an oxymoron, it cannot be done. However, in surplus reality it can happen. Psyche and matter are not divided on stage. There we experience the transformation: I am you, you are me.

DAG: Do you use the word 'essence' also in a spiritual sense?

ZERKA: It can be understood both ways, in a physical and a spiritual sense. When you do a role reversal you can suddenly feel your body changing, your whole being transforms itself. It transcends, it goes beyond that old self that was facing this person and becomes another. In the sharing phase, auxiliary egos often reveal bodily experiences when sharing from the role they just took which the protagonist finds staggeringly accurate. Thus, the auxiliaries reach action insight.

When you are an auxiliary ego or double to the protagonist you have to obliterate the prior perception you held of that person. If that does not happen you have not done a complete role reversal. That is precisely why in some psychodramas the role reversal does not work. It is theatrical psychodramatic discipline, which is crucial in psychodrama. To quote Stanislavski: 'Learn to love the role in yourself, not yourself in the role'.

Let me draw the following conclusion from what I said: when a so-called projection is a reality for the protagonist, it is rather un-therapeutic on the psychodrama stage to refer to this perception as a 'projection'. Maybe the following example will serve. A young male patient presents himself to Moreno because he has been seeing a non-directive therapist without any results. He found himself unable to speak to the therapist. At the time of his very first therapeutic session he became completely mute and subsequent sessions did not change that behaviour. Moreno asked him to set up that very first encounter with his former therapist and suggested to the patient that he soliloquize his thoughts and feelings. The young man begins with his head slightly turned aside, apparently unable to look at the therapist. Moreno encourages him again and now he begins to speak: 'Today is Wednesday. He is wearing a blue shirt. Everybody knows that homosexuals wear blue shirts on a Wednesday to signal to other homosexuals that they are available.' This is where the psychodramatic treatment began. It is evident that the poor non-directive therapist did not know how directive he was to this patient without even speaking a word. That was the patient's *reality*, not a *projection*.

DAG: It is quite common, particularly in group psychotherapy, that group members as well as therapists point out to others that they are projecting. Accurate critique towards the therapist can thus be interpreted as a father or mother projection or a problem with authority figures. That point of view removes the therapist from the patient's reality. To explain a client's behaviour by the phenomenon of projection means to neglect how things appear to the client. In this manner you actually convey to the patient that *your* reality perception is superior to his/hers.

Therapists would probably lose their business if the term 'projection' ceased to have meaning. In psychotherapy projection is the goose that lays the golden eggs.

A prerequisite for being a director of psychodrama and for directing any protagonist is to leave one's own opinions aside as much as possible. Of course, one's perception is to a great extent created by attitudes, feelings and opinions and vice versa, but they should be held flexibly as they may be influenced and changed by the client's self-presentation. Therefore, a director should not see this as a disadvantage or a handicap. It could as well be a resource because of the dramatic tension between protagonist and director. To respect the protagonist is of critical importance.

ZERKA: I may say to the protagonist: 'Do you want to hear what my perception of this is? Would you like to hear it? I differ from you in this and that respect, but I am not you. I still have to respect your perception. But this is what I see. Is it possible that what I see is correct or is it incorrect? We can clarify it together.'

DAG: That is very modest and a healing way of approaching it because it still gives the protagonist a chance to say: 'No, this is the way I perceive it'.

ZERKA: *Affirmation comes before negation.* First affirm the protagonist. Once they are affirmed they can change! If you push persons with their backs against the wall, what do they want to do? They want to strike out, they want to fight, they want to resist you. Or they go under, they duck, they disappear.

DAG: From a classical psychoanalytic point of view, one may say that projection is connected to strong emotional reactions. People get very angry, sad, bitter, or even paranoid. How do you work when you see that in the group, for example in the sharing?

ZERKA: I can usually explain best by giving an example. I get as a protagonist a man who has made a suicide attempt. In psychodrama we work through his depression, the reason for his attempt and his determination to live. In the sharing a woman who had been his auxiliary ego wife suddenly turned upon him violently and said, 'I hope you are happy now that you have made a suicide attempt. I suppose you are going to do it again!' I stopped her and said, 'Wait a minute, you were this man's wife before in the psychodrama. He picked you for the role and mentioned in the sharing that you were one of his best friends in the clinic here. He also showed us his determination to go on with his life, so whom are you talking to?' She burst out, pointed to the protagonist and said: 'Him'. I interjected 'No. No, you are not talking to this man now. Whom out there are you addressing?' I pointed to the window. She began to cry and said, 'Oh my God, I just realized my brother committed suicide two years ago'. I put my arm around her shoulder, 'Lady, there is your concern, you have unfinished business with your brother which you are putting upon this man. The protagonist has nothing to do with it, he did not actually commit suicide, although he was deeply depressed. Clearly, he is not going to do it again, we all saw that today.'

When I see that kind of unreasonable emotion I do not call it projection; it is emotion inappropriately directed to a person who should not be receiving it. In short: you can define projection as an *inadequate emotional response* directed towards another object, person or matter, in a specific situation. This is opposite to spontaneity where the emotional response would be adequate and in accordance with the situation.

DAG: The psychodrama stage does not differentiate inside–outside, fantasy–reality, past–present–future. Because there is no need for ego to make this differentiation the whole phenomenon of projection really does not have any validity in the psychodramatic context. Where there is participation mystique or archaic identification the idea of projection is invalid.

ZERKA: In the psychodrama we work with what is presented and whether it is a projection or not is unimportant. The relationship is a fluid. The question one asks oneself is, 'Where do I place myself on this continuum with this person?' Placing myself in the loving context is one position, placing myself in an antagonistic context is another. There is where the boundaries can be specified and worked through, the place on the continuum, but otherwise it is very fluid.

DAG: Moreno did not refer to the phenomenon of projection (and transference) in his books very often, for which he was criticized by psychoanalysts. He did not seem to be of the opinion that these phenomena were a *via regia* to the psyche.

We in Western cultures have the tendency to look upon other cultures as primitive because they believe that nature has a soul. What is your point of view about the Western disregard for the belief that the world has a soul? Can the world soul only be seen as a projection phenomenon?

ZERKA: For Native Americans the earth and everything in it has spirits. The Finns have this furry tree-trunk with a face, it is considered the spirit of the tree. We do not have to go as far as Africa, we find it in Europe too. This mythology has to be respected, lived and worked through. The German psychodrama students love to work with fairy tales. What are these fairy tales? We give weight to figures that never were, never will be, but which play a part in our creative lives and our imagination. These are realities on a different level. For Moreno it is important that the psychodramatist be a combination of artist and scientist. The artist understands this. In art we are required to suspend critical judgement. Except for the earlier Jungian psychotherapists, many, especially psychoanalytically oriented ones, have divorced themselves from this mythology.

DAG: Let me read a sentence from the book *The Early Greek Concept of the Soul*:

> in Homer's time the individual did not yet know of the will as an ethical factor, nor did he distinguish between what was inside and outside himself as we do. When referring to themselves, the early Greeks, like other Indo-European peoples, did not primarily consider themselves to be independent individuals but rather members of a group.
>
> (Bremmer 1983: 67)

I was always impressed by how both you and J.L. Moreno stressed healthy interdependence rather then independence. As a human being, living in a human society, we are all interdependent. From this perspective independence is both impossible and unhealthy. The overestimation of independence as a sign of a healthy individual can be misleading. It can create either a great regression, turning an adult into a demanding child or into a psychopath. One may therefore conclude that it could well be helpful for people nowadays in Western societies to develop more trust in dependence as a therapeutic goal. In another society, as for example India, with its overemphasis on dependence, there the opposite is desirable. Protagonists in India often put on stage subjects like arranged marriages, submission to the family and the group, and the right of women to go to work and achieve some economic independence. In short, I believe that the opposite of being dependent is healthy interdependence.

Chapter 14

Group psychotherapy and the individual

These thoughts lead us to the concept of group psychotherapy. In group psychotherapy the group comes first, the individual comes second. The focus is on involvement and belonging, on aspects of relationships. A relationship by definition involves two or more persons. The need for belonging is a universal human trait. Drawings of social atoms have shown that this belonging does not necessarily mean that the biological family is the first choice, which indicates that the family is only one form of group formation.

Moreno did not place the individual and the group in opposition. His prime concern was the creation of tele between the individuals in the group. From a Morenian point of view the group does not have a conscious or unconscious of its own, as some group analysts claim. A group consists of individual human beings and their relationships to one another. These relationships are formed of mutual attractions and rejections which become the basis of group awareness and consciousness.

Being a member of a group brings up problems of ethics and concern as well as conscience. Conscience, like shame, throws us into a condition of tension and includes an awareness of the other. It has an aspect of justice, that is, one takes the other into account as much as oneself. Therefore, it is of an anti-ego character, it does not serve the ego's immediate interests. It means restrictions, which work against impulsivity and instinctive ruthlessness, enabling spontaneous behaviour. We sacrifice the impulse because of love for someone else or some ideal. This aspect of the justice of conscience is most important. It is the basis for love towards the other and oneself. It was this love that freed us from barbaric or titanic behaviour and which makes us human with an ability to reflect, to respect boundaries and create forms.

Conscience is pluralistic, which means it rarely expresses itself in only one voice or opinion but rather in several. One aspect of conscience is of

Apollonian nature, which acts like a superego in the Freudian sense and is to a great extent learned through one's individual and collective history. This aspect of conscience reflects spiritual and moral ideas and is the foundation of our society's ethics, norms, rules and laws. Crimes against this aspect of our conscience often lead to fear of exclusion from the collective, producing feelings of guilt and atonement. In that sense, confession as practised in many Christian denominations is a way to be forgiven for one's sins and signals permission to return to the group. In group psychotherapy we also experience this by opening ourselves up to the others, revealing our darker sides and experiencing the cathartic effect and relief of being readmitted to the group.

Group psychotherapy deals with individuals 'in' the group. As group psychotherapists we often see the individual's dilemma in that how they want to relate to other people is not always the way their words and actions are perceived. It may very well be that an individual has a great understanding of his or her own needs and desires and how he or she wants to live. This is rather commonly found in the introvert whose desires and needs may not fit in with those of others. Psychotic behaviour in psychiatric patients would be an example of extremely unspontaneous behaviour since they cannot convey themselves meaningfully to their environment. On the psychodrama stage these patients are encouraged to give their world substance and enact their way of perceiving it. The group members can then participate in this 'hallucinatory world' and through this participation it becomes less threatening for them. When this stage is reached in the therapeutic process even the protagonist's 'word salad' diminishes. The patient's relationship to the group and the group's relationship to the 'delusionary world' is the therapeutic agent. Thus psychodrama builds bridges between different worlds, peoples, religions, and, as seen above, to a behaviour that at first seemed unfamiliar and strange.

ZERKA: Let us look at the child. I think most children before the age of 5 are aware that they come from the cosmos. They are part of the universe.

DAG: Not from mom and dad or the stork?

ZERKA: The soul is aware that the child has come from somewhere else. I have a childhood memory of coming out of some darkness into comparative light. Whether it was the moment of birth or whether a moment of awareness of dark and light I do not know. I think this moment of being in that twilight zone is still being connected to the cosmos. Then you suddenly discover that you no longer are connected to the cosmos. You are connected to material things, a person coming, going. Moreno described this in his chapter on child development. Because we come from the cosmos we think we are the entire world: children are gifted with 'normal megalomania' that they never quite lose and sometimes apply to themselves as a therapeutic instrument. Somehow our neurological structure perpetuates that idea. You and I say goodnight to each other and there is a moon. You go left to the hotel, I go right to the car. I look up, the moon goes with me. You look up, the moon goes with you. Each individual has a thread to the moon, like a balloon. It is as if you are pulling the moon with you, but I feel the moon comes with me. Yet it is the same moon. Our cosmic awareness is that there is only one moon, but we are each individually connected to it, which makes it appear as if there were two moons. Again we come to time and space. The cosmic being, the child, becomes aware of material beings around itself and it takes a long time before it knows it is a member of a group because different people around it come and go. Then they begin to recognize these different people.

DAG: Do you think group awareness comes first?

ZERKA: No, while a child you are totally dependent on other people and that makes you a member of a group. Even if it is only a dyad, mother and child, it is already a small group. The smallest unit of social interaction is the pair. But awareness comes later.

We do not consider persons in Western cultures as adults until they have totally individuated, which means that they are themselves, independent, competent to care for themselves, and we emphasize that and push them towards isolation. They lose contact with the family of origin and may even lose contact with the cosmos. There are many rich things in Western culture, but much impoverishment too. Listen to how the Russians talk about mother earth, or to the Native Americans who believe that the earth is their mother. We in the Western cultures have lost that feeling for the Great Mother.

DAG: When did Moreno introduce the term 'group psychotherapy'?

ZERKA: Moreno started with group psychotherapy in 1912 when he began to work with the prostitutes of Vienna. They belonged to a very specific group in that they were isolated and rejected – in a word, pariahs. He was concerned that this particular group of people, by virtue of the fact that they were sexual providers, were made into a separate group from the rest of society. Prostitutes were rejected by the Catholic church; the church wanted them to become good girls, to reform them into respectable, God-fearing citizens; the Marxists rejected them because they considered them bad citizens. Everybody rejected them. They could not get a doctor or medical care and they could not get a lawyer if they were beaten up by a client. Moreno saw them as totally defenceless as a group. His wish was not to transform them into respectable citizens, he wanted to help them be more cohesive, to help one another. He defined group psychotherapy as every person being the therapeutic agent of the other, one group as the therapeutic agent of the other. He wanted to help them to help themselves and to teach them self-respect for what they were doing.

The curious thing is that when the First World War broke out, the whole prostitution business began to change because the soldiers wanted prostitutes or maybe some of them became respectable, but the whole culture erupted. He did not follow up the group of prostitutes further, since he was drafted into the medical branch of the Austrian army.

Before the end of that war Moreno was appointed superintendent of a refugee camp, Mittendorf. The refugees consisted of Austrian citizens who had lived close to the Italian border and were assumed to be loyal to the enemy, the Italian population. Indeed, they spoke Italian and their occupation was that of wine growers. In the camp they were turned into factory workers, a totally foreign employment for them. Again he faced groups of uprooted persons, the helpless, the young, the aged, women and children, all of whom were forcibly moved from one location to another. The men had been taken away to the war. Moreno wanted to give them a sense of belonging. He observed what was happening, he saw women at the mercy of the male guards; they had no husbands or brothers to protect them, their own men were old and went to sleep. He felt responsible for those who were helpless, and vulnerable. He saw that in psychotics later as well: helplessness and vulnerability.

It was in Mittendorf that he developed his ideas about sociometry, which he meant to use to reorganize the groups and empower the population. The empowerment he intended to introduce was to give the women the opportunity to choose their housemates, their co-workers and even the guards. He wanted to build a community based on sociometric principles. Regrettably the authorities did not give him that permission. As it was wartime the authorities needed especially to keep what they considered law and order and were afraid to give people the power to shape their own lives.

DAG: So Mittendorf was another beginning of the concept of group psychotherapy which he later developed in his practice as a psychiatrist. One individual could be a therapeutic, serving or helping agent for another. When do you think he first used the term 'group psychotherapy' in a clinical sense?

ZERKA: When he went to work in Sing Sing prison in 1931. He was invited by Warden Lawes, superintendent, to come to the prison to turn it into a socialized community. Moreno studied the personalities of the inmates, made a sociometric evaluation and then had them put together as complementary or as similar personalities so they could help one another. Many of these inmates were heavily disturbed or if they were not in the beginning the isolation on every level and the condition in the prison produced such disturbances sooner or later. That was how Moreno turned this prison into a socialized community. On the basis of that study he was invited to come to The New York State Training School for Girls in Hudson, New York in 1932, where he began to collect data for his magnum opus *Who Shall Survive?* and also to explore various other school systems.

He never believed that group psychotherapy by itself could heal, he never believed that sociometry on its own could heal, neither did he believe that psychodrama alone was the healing agent. They had to come together under an overall umbrella. It was a threefold sociometric system: all components are intended to be used together. *He never planned for psychodrama to be separated from the others.*

When he began to work with patients of his own, psychodrama became the focus. This was somewhat contrary to his original intention, which was to create a sociometric revolution in which people not only helped themselves, but had the freedom to move around and find new alliances as their sociometric criteria changed. He believed everyone should be allowed to choose with whom they wanted to live, learn, work, play, and have all manner of meaningful interactions.

Chapter 15

The protagonist

Traditional and classical theatre is built upon conflicts such as treachery, betrayal, jealousy, love, marriage, stepmothers, death, inheritance. In the Greek dramas the protagonist is either the cause for what happens to him or her because of hubris, misunderstanding or carelessness, or they are simply thrown into the events by fate, the gods' desire for entertainment, or a spell cast by the Delphic oracle. Protagonists like Oedipus, Orestes and Electra have not necessarily done anything to deserve their fate. The protagonist's task is to try to manage the situation in the best way possible. His/her dialogues mirror thoughts and feelings through the chorus. It is the tension within the dialogues which is the object of the dramatic production. The drama dealt with how the human beings coped with their mundane instincts and limits and their relationship to the gods. In the Greek drama we follow the protagonist's dialogues and destiny for better or worse.

In psychodrama it is that tension and bringing it onto the stage which builds the drama. Therein lies the beauty: the tension in every moment of the spontaneous production, every moment in itself, will reveal that 'beauty'. Even the most painful scenes in psychodrama contain that particular protagonist's unique dilemma.

The Greek word 'protagonist' consists of two parts: protos, *which means 'first', and* agon *which means 'to be, to do, to act'. Before he was an actor he was the central figure, the main character, number one in the Dionysian ritual, as well as in the Olympic games, such as the discus thrower. Because the Olympic games were competitive, every protagonist had an antagonist. However, Moreno did not use the word 'antagonist' for auxiliary egos. It is not a good idea to use this word, because there is more than antagonism between protagonist and auxiliary ego even though they may be in a fight now and then. The auxiliary ego is not, in principle, an antagonist, but a therapeutic agent.*

The protagonist in psychodrama is analogous to that in the earlier pre-ancient Greek drama. There he was the protagonist, the author, the performer and the director. In later developments of the drama these roles were separated and handed over to different persons. The dramas were now directed, rehearsed and performed and were no longer spontaneous, even if performed only once. In later dramas the protagonist emerged out of the chorus and the written drama became a dialogue between the protagonist and the chorus.

The word 'protagonist' may also mean 'first in agony'. Since Moreno took this word from the Greek theatre, we can assume that he meant to imply that the protagonist in a psychodrama is also going through a Dionysian journey. This journey is first and foremost characterized by humiliation, shame and death in a land of horror and fear; he or she is facing danger on their own. It is a lonely meeting with death. Death is here seen in the sense of 'life cannot go on like this'. The status quo is gone when Dionysus appears.

Moreno founded his idea of spontaneity and creativity on the confrontation with the moment of surprise, which could be likened to the appearance of Dionysus. Moreno's idea of 'the psychology of the moment' dealt with the moment of creativity in which no warnings were given in advance and no predictions could be made. Things just happen: one gets fired, divorced, someone dies; everything happens without warning. Even if the death of someone close was long foreseen, Dionysus still enters the scene when this person really dies. It is still a moment of surprise and shock.

*When people ask, 'What can I do to prevent this or that from happening?' or 'What can I do to feel as I did before this happened to me?', the answer is: 'Nothing!' This moment of surprise involves no return. It has already happened. It arouses confusion, fear and pity, and initiates the divine madness (*Theia Mania*). Such a moment can trigger anxiety, which is the opposite of spontaneity; the latter leads to mastering the situation adequately. Moreno was of the opinion that the ego was very badly prepared for surprises and meets a new situation with a lack of spontaneity. In psychodrama the protagonist can rediscover and recover spontaneity.*

People constantly search for explanations, but like natural catastrophes many experiences remain unexplainable. Suffering and pain are not always the results of outside influences. Sometimes they may not even be the result of inner influences, they just happen.

What is characteristic for the god Dionysus is movement, not remaining in a situation where one is left hanging, where one is stuck. Moreno put much emphasis on the idea of moving on. Movement away from stagnation will always involve anxiety, and possibly fear or other emotions.

It is a common error to understand psychodrama only as a method of 'dissonance reduction' in order to 'cure the person'. True healing implies the inclusion of all aspects, in order to give meaning to them.

If psychodrama is to follow the psychotherapeutic tradition, i.e., to serve the soul, then honour must be given to the need to follow the Dionysian process of disintegration with ultimate re-connection between life and soul. All of this hinges on giving honour to dissonance by experiencing it. Moreno once said that psychodrama was the therapy for fallen gods.

DAG: Do you know when Moreno started to use the word 'protagonist'?

ZERKA: Aristotle's *De Poetica*, especially his description of catharsis in the spectator, influenced him. Aristotle claimed that catharsis in people watching a tragedy involves especially two emotions: pity and fear. In some translations in English it is awe and fear. Aristotle believed that spectators identify with the main character – Oedipus, for example. This means that Oedipus, the protagonist, carries these emotions on behalf of the spectators who, by watching him, achieve an emotional purge because they share these experiences with Oedipus: they feel terror and pity, awe and pity for his tragic development.

Because Moreno was particularly interested in action and the position of the actor, he said that the spectators knew very well that the figure on stage was not really Oedipus, it was a representation of his story. Behind the mask of Oedipus there was a real person, an actor. What are the actors feelings in relation to the roles they are playing? What is really going on in this person? If we removed the mask, what would we see? What effect would it have upon the spectators to watch this person's own pain, fears, terrors, joys? Moreno called this identification with the protagonist an 'aesthetic catharsis'.

What Moreno was aiming for was a *personal therapeutic catharsis*. This was a genuine revolution in the theatre. Very few people understand this revolution of the spontaneous actor not being a Harlequin, a clown, a nobleman, or the Virgin Mary, which are still representations of beings other than themselves. He wanted the actor to be him- or herself, revealing him- or herself as they really are with their limitations, their choices, their fears, in every sense. Moreno taught us to let them be their own protagonist instead of the protagonist of a role ascribed to them, either by a dramatic adviser or a writer, however great a genius; that has nothing to do with it. We do not detract from that, it is a different process. I want to know what this person is really feeling on his or her own behalf. Then I can say that in the group observing this, people watching this, there will be a personal therapeutic catharsis because these are real fears, real tears, real laughter, real joy.

Moreno discovered among actors a particular kind of professional disease such as waiters who get flat feet and miners who get miner's lung. Actors get what he called *histrionic neurosis*. They are a little piece of other people's psyches via the roles they play. For example, Oedipus, Hamlet, King Lear, Macbeth, stick to their psyches and reduce or fight with their own creativity. They often become very disturbed, drink, become addicts of all sorts, have terrible private lives. What he wanted to do was to restore the creativity of the actor, not of the role.

DAG: How do you think we should relate to the rule that we should follow the protagonist's truth?

ZERKA: We worked with a young man of about 18 years of age who had fallen in love with his older stepbrother. Mother and father had divorced and remarried, it was a blended family, with several sons in the family. The two youngest boys started sexual relations in their teens. The stepbrother was about three or four years older than the protagonist. By the time our protagonist, our patient, was 18 years old the other boy had moved to a heterosexual level, stopped their relationship and brought a girlfriend home. This made our friend very, very ill. He developed the idea that he was now pregnant with his lover's child as he considered them a married pair with our patient playing the role of the wife who believed he/she was pregnant. He was brought to us in this agitated, pseudo-pregnant state.

Moreno began by exploring in action the relationship between these two young men and the rejection Micky received from his lover. It was a very sad story. At the same time our patient was really a nasty little boy. He was very manipulative. There is hardly a greater manipulation than for a wife to accuse her husband, now unfaithful, that he is deserting her while she is pregnant with their child, when in fact she is not.

Three times he went from the state, where the family lived, to New York City, to a hotel, checked in and called his mother long-distance to say that he was going to commit suicide in the hotel. If that was not manipulative I would not know what is. On one hand I saw this manipulative, nasty little character, on the other hand I saw his pain. Without asking the protagonist, Moreno assigned me as his double and told me to go on stage. Doubling was my major function at that time in the theatre. From the moment I left my seat in the audience where I had been sitting as a spectator to the moment I stepped upon the stage and stood next to him, I was transformed from a person who looked at this person and said he is a suffering but nasty character, to a person who is just suffering. We began to talk about our pain and how we could ever live and make peace with this.

Imagine being in the role of this young man, experiencing this rejection and all that it implies. We are exposing the pain without comment. That is the last scene in that particular psychodrama.

In later psychodramas we dealt specifically with his relationship to his former lover and their families. But at this point Moreno stopped the psychodrama to impress upon the group how much our patient was suffering, so that the nurses, the other students, the staff and the other patients would be gentle with him and would not laugh or scoff at him and say to him: 'You are not pregnant, boys cannot conceive'. No, he did not touch that at all. He touched upon the agony.

I sit back down among the group and Moreno begins to take Micky out of the psychodrama, back to the group, to build bridges, and to explain to the group: 'You have seen what happened, you have seen how much he suffers'. At some point he starts to speak to the protagonist who is sitting next to him and who begins to shake his head negatively. Moreno asks: 'What is the matter?' The protagonist points to me and says: 'You explain me to him'. What happened is that I had been inside of him, all the others were outside of him. Only I could understand and feel with him.

After this first session the young man did not bring his idea about the baby up any more. He just needed to be heard, to be known, to be seen, to be felt, to be affirmed and respected.

DAG: That has been my experience with psychodrama also, with both healthy and disturbed people. As long as they bring the action and their agony on the stage they start to see the situation from within their own agony, creating a different perspective. To bring that about is the artistry of the director. As a director you role-reverse with both the protagonist and the significant others on the stage, you operate within the distance, the in-between, the agony within the protagonist is what you dramatize on the stage. In a sense you could say this tension between the protagonist and his significant other sets the scene. If these dialogues are properly enacted on the stage, I have always experienced that the symptoms disappear.

ZERKA: I agree. At one time people used to say to Moreno, 'You are treating the symptom, but are you treating the disease?' He replied, 'If you tell me how I can separate the symptom from the disease I would be very happy'. The symptom is where we psychodramatists start. But we do not leave it there. Some others would say, 'You make patients sicker, you confirm them in their sickness'. Moreno answered, 'Yes, in a way, I give them a dose of insanity under conditions of control and safety'. Psychodrama is a homeopathic remedy (*Simile similis curantur*). But he also said, 'It's not the insanity I worry about, it is the control. Here the control is therapeutic, in the world at large the control is dangerous, anti-therapeutic and punitive.'

DAG: Moreno stated very clearly that the purpose of surplus reality is to liberate the human from the chain of reality. Psychodrama can give people an experience they cannot have in the world outside the psychodrama theatre: for example, to commit suicide and still be alive afterwards, or be an 18-year-old pregnant man as in your example. Here on the stage he can act out and encounter his world. In giving his world substance he will become the creator together with other group members because now in the psychodrama he is no longer alone. He brings other participants into his world.

ZERKA: We may first have to give protagonists a double to help them to deepen the experience of the agony and widen it, to increase it. That is what people meant when they said, 'You make patients sicker'. Another of Moreno's responses was, 'Yes, I do. I bring height, depth, and width to their problem, over and beyond what they can do by themselves. If they could do this by themselves they would not need us.'

When referring to his work with psychotic patients, Moreno would say that a psychotic patient is creating an inner birth process: s/he is creating a new identity for him- or herself. The patient cannot do it alone because nobody listens, nobody takes him/her seriously, or nobody understands. A protagonist needs an audience. You and I have an audience with each other.

The psychotic has no audience and is driven further and further into isolation because nobody believes him: 'You are not Jesus Christ, your name is Bill Brown!' That is what the analyst does. Moreno, on the contrary, would say, 'Jesus, I've always wanted to meet you. You had such a fascinating life. Show me what it is like!' What we become here as therapists and psychodrama directors are midwives, to bring this unfinished birth to completion. Once it is completed the protagonist can look at it from a greater distance. Can you imagine what would happen to a woman who would always be pregnant and never see or hold her baby? She would go crazy. What keeps us tied to life is unfinished business. The psychotic has enormous unfinished business, s/he is incapable of completing it by him-/herself. S/he needs the midwife, the therapist, to bring it to birth. This birth process takes place in surplus reality together with the director and the group, in the magical world of psychodrama. Then, perhaps, the protagonist can learn to separate from the psychotic structure. Not until that happens can s/he get well.

Chapter 16

Sociometry

Regrettably, there is a tendency in group psychotherapy to apply ideas about the group which predate the advent of sociometry. Frequently the approach to group psychotherapy follows ideas related to and rooted in psychoanalysis and the psychology of the unconscious, of the individual, rather than to those which are guided by group dynamics as revealed through sociometry. The healing process in psychoanalysis is related to the dissolution of the projection phenomena manifested in the transference process towards the therapist and the members of the group.

Moreno emphasized that the therapeutic agency was not necessarily related to the therapist, but that it was inherent in every member of the group. Sociometry deals with choices. Because they are usually written down or made in action, the choices are always conscious The motivation for the choice – the rationale, feelings and needs as presented by the group members – gives all the insight that is needed. There may well be unconscious motivation for choices but once they are declared and voiced they are no longer unconscious. The sociogram makes choices visible, facilitating the group psychotherapeutic process which includes encounter and psychodrama.

To work in groups in which only transference is recognized as motivation is to work with what 'is not manifest'. Therefore, transference relies on interpretation. The interpretation has to be accepted and agreed upon if it is to have any therapeutic value. In psychoanalysis as well as group analysis, the mutual agreement on interpretation is critical and many times the reason that therapies reach an abrupt end. Sociometry forces the group members to deal with the reality of their choices, whatever they may be.

Sociometric studies have pointed out that an individual's standing in the group may not have as much to do with personality as with level of acceptance and mutual regard. It is mutuality of positive choices that makes for group cohesion and group effectiveness. That is best built by allowing people to express and act upon their choices.

Sociometry is an umbrella concept which deals with the essence of the human encounter in a rich variety of roles and counter-roles.

DAG: On the psychodrama stage we are dealing with the protagonist's life, with his or her perception of their inner and outer world. When working with their social atom we are looking at both these worlds.

The protagonist's social atom is always perceived from this point of view and is, therefore, subjective and one-sided. Sociometry, on the contrary, deals with mutual choices within a group and is at least two-sided. How would you define sociometry?

ZERKA: Sociometry deals with human relationships in terms of role interactions with significant others on the private level, on the professional level and on the community level. It was one of Moreno's ideas that there is too much forcing people into relationships which are not mutually productive and that we would do far better if we allowed people to have their choices even if that meant that choices might be changed. When choices change it is because our role interactions change. There should be enough flexibility built into the system to allow for that.

We make poor choices for partners in marriage, one of the central foci in our lives, or for mates or lovers. In childhood we are not allowed to practise choosing sufficiently and if you do not allow the child or a person to practise what they need to practise they lose that capacity. An educator by the name of Makarenko, who worked with orphans left by the convulsions of the revolution in Russia, stated: 'If you want a child to be courageous, put that child into situations where it can practise courage'. Perhaps what psychology and psychiatry tend to overlook is some basic knowledge that pedagogues can contribute to the developmental aspects of the human being. Moreno was also an excellent pedagogue, as witnessed by his improvisational drama groups made up of the children in the gardens of Vienna while he was still a student of philosophy.

We influenced the military during the Second World War. This is described in our volume *Group Psychotherapy: A Symposium*, published in 1945, and incidentally, the first book ever to carry that title. The British found that when that war broke out, there were not enough officers for the conscription army. Britain had a volunteer army whose officers came mainly from the upper strata of society or it was a hereditary function. With conscription and the entrance of so many soldiers, there were not enough officers. The military had two ways of assigning men to officer candidacy school; one was to have a board of superior officers pick men from among the ranks, those they felt were suitable to become officers. The other was influenced by Moreno's idea that peers should choose from among their peers, so they allowed this to happen as well. That meant there were two groups: *superior-assigned* and *peer-assigned*. They followed them up to see how they fared when they went into battle. What did they find? Those who had been picked by their peers fared much better in terms of the troops' recognition of their leadership, their ability to coordinate their troops, their survival rate; all these were superior to those who had been picked by their superior officers. Here you have a perfect confirmation of Moreno's idea for building good group cohesion: give people the freedom of choice. (Moreno 1945: 205–217)

DAG: Choice is, therefore, a central subject in sociometric and psychodramatic philosophy?

ZERKA: Sharing time and space with other humans are dynamic categories of living. We cannot escape that. Some of us have lived in families we did not want to be in, sharing time and space with them. Some believe that we make that choice before birth. At times we may think we made a poor choice, the task of learning is so hard. That's why we have so much therapy, to make up for the difficult choices. For others it is a very productive choice, to learn what they need to learn for their soul.

DAG: What is the exact meaning of the word 'sociometry'?

ZERKA: Measurement of human relations. That's the simplest way to state it. *Socius* is a Latin word and *métron* is of Greek origin. *Socius* means 'fellow, companion along the way' and there you have it already: who is your companion along the way? It is someone with whom you are doing something in common. *Métron* means 'to measure'. In sociometry we measure human contact and interaction.

DAG: The Latin word *societas* had a very clear and distinct meaning and designated a formation where people came together for certain purposes, e.g. to master a situation such as toppling a king or to carry out a crime. The ASGPP (American Society of Group Psychotherapy and Psychodrama) would be such a *societas*, where people come together under the common criterion of their interest in psychodrama and group psychotherapy.

Sociometry deals with the mutuality of choices within the organization. So one can say that any society has a criterion as its topic and sociometry deals with how people choose one another around a specific criterion. *Sociometry is action-oriented, focused on a common activity to be carried out by the group members.*

ZERKA: It is meant to change the world, to change, improve and enrich human interactions on all levels, wherever those may be.

DAG: I think it is important to point out that sociometry, like society, has action as its goal; after that goal is reached and completed the next action comes up. It is like a circle: the completion of one and the beginning of a new action.

ZERKA: We have the rise of a certain goal into action, the fulfilment, productivity and completion. We may have a decline, a death if it is no longer functional.

DAG: Could we say that sociometry deals with the group and the outer world?

ZERKA: Yes. It is given in the words 'companion along the way'.

DAG: When did Moreno actually produce his first sociometric research?

ZERKA: In the New York State Training School for Girls at Hudson. But he also did his research in various other schools, so chronologically it is not clear whether the Hudson work came first or whether the research elsewhere was done concurrently. Historically, it was immediately after his work at Sing Sing Prison in 1931. He was appointed Director of Research at Hudson, New York in 1932, and also in the early 30s he was permitted to enter various school systems and apply sociometry there in classes from kindergarten on up.

In Sing Sing he began first with what he called 'the assignment technique'. There he was a researcher getting to know the prisoners, putting them together in cells in ways which made them compatible and therapeutic with one another, to turn it into a therapeutic community. The idea was that while they were in prison they would learn and gain something from one another, not merely be punished, but learn something about being human. This learning they could also use when they left the stifling prison environment and were allowed to grow. It is a very liberal view, of course: moral re-education.

Moreno's concern was that children be permitted to make choices and he observed how well they would do that. For instance, studying children in the kindergarten, what did he discover? Their choices are very hit-or-miss, their sense for mutuality is not yet refined, it develops with age. That is why you see so many one-way choices in the sociogram of that age group, very little reciprocity. *What is important is mutuality*, choosing each other for the same interaction at the same time. You chose me to do this book together, I chose you to do this book together; I could not have done it with anyone else in the same way, you could not have done it with anybody else. *That is profound mutuality*. It does not always work in that unique fashion, sometimes it does. It is said that Gilbert and Sullivan, who wrote so many charming operetta-type productions together, could not stand each other, but only on this criterion of 'producing a piece of light drama with music together' were they able to cooperate. Apparently when they split up their partnership, neither was as productive alone as they had been together.

Another example of recognition of positive role interactions was my son Jonathan who, at age 3, pointed out to me a number of his play-school playmates: 'That one is good for building blocks with, that one plays fireman with me, that one is for colouring books with', etc. – a set of role diagrams in action. I believe Jonathan's early experience with psychodrama helped that kind of awareness.

In the Gilbert and Sullivan story we find a very special form of role interaction; in the Jonathan tale we find a rather mature consciousness of role interaction in a young child. There are also people who make choices on a different basis, for instance, a husband who chooses his wife absolutely and is faithful to her, but he is not enough for the wife: she needs other companions, a father or lover; so even on the level of choice capacity and maintaining loyalty to that choice we vary enormously.

As children mature, an increase in the number of choices which are reciprocated at the same time, in the same place and on the same criterion can be noted, and that is central in sociometry.

DAG: A sociogram is always done in the here and now. It is future-oriented as it gives birth to future actions.

ZERKA: You can only survey the past from your own perception because usually the significant others of the past situation are not present. But even if they were, their subjective perception of that past may well be at variance from your own. I recall a scene with my mother years ago. I had started to write some of my youthful memories of our family. Without my knowledge, she picked up my papers, read them, and told me: 'I do not recognize myself here'. My response was: 'That's OK, Mum, these are my memoirs, not yours. You will write yours from your perspective.' On the other hand, when I showed another segment to my sister, her eyes became teary and she whispered: 'It's beautiful and that is just the way it was'. Probably seen from the point of view of the same generation, however different the placement in the birth rank and personality, there is greater conformity of perception and experience. But all of it depends upon subjective perception.

With sociometry as an aid, one can also look at some choices you would want to make in the future. A clear example of this happened in Beacon in the late 40s. Moreno had employed an African-American head nurse at the sanatorium. She proved to be the best psychiatric nurse we ever had. Some experiences with the position of head nurses in our hospital had taught us that certain hierarchical positions tend to isolate the person who occupies that position, no matter what the personality. One can see it in business and administration and unless that person is able to establish a firm mutual relationship with another in that organization this position is made extremely difficult.

That summer we enrolled a Japanese student. As part of the training, we carried out a sociometric test on the criterion: 'With whom do you want to spend a free evening while you are here?' The nurse and the student chose each other mutually; they made no other choices. When the student completed her stay with us and departed, Moreno pulled out the sociogram and pointed to it. He shook his head and looked worried. Then he confided in me: 'Miss B is an excellent head nurse, the entire staff likes her. There has been no problem with her and she is so good with the patients. But I predict that since our Japanese student left, we are going to lose Miss B in a few weeks. Look here, she has lost her first and only choice.' He turned out to be completely accurate: Miss B gave notice two weeks later. Moreno described this type of interpersonal connection, an exclusive one, as 'aristo-tele'. He defines 'aristo-tele' as a person of high hierarchic standing who has an exclusive mutual choice with a sociometric leader. The word *aristo* comes from the Greek and means 'best'. Aristocracy refers to a class of persons holding exceptional rank and privileges.

DAG: Is a criterion always a precondition for a sociometric choice?

ZERKA: Yes, the criterion is the compass for the role and vice versa. Role interactions belong to different criteria. After all, just as we are multiple role players, we are also multiple criteria carriers, that's what we do not realize. One of the most profound difficulties with monogamy is that we are multiple criteria people and if I choose a partner who does not have a role repertoire that fits my role repertoire we are in profound trouble. Then, even assuming that person has the role, if I do not play it the way my partner needs it and he does not play it the way I need it, just having the same role is not sufficient. We need to be able to perform it in a way which is mutually harmonious to be productive, otherwise it becomes counter-productive. That's why I think so many of our marriages fail.

Before you were married or chose a mate, or lived with someone, you had eight, nine or ten friends, each of whom fitted a different role interaction and a different criterion. Now somehow society tells you: 'You can't do that any more. You have chosen this person to live with, now this person has to fulfil all your criteria.' It doesn't work well. Why do our marriages break down? I believe because monogamy is sociometrically contraindicated. I think it is not for the masses, but it is for a small *aristocracy*, for people who can maintain that exclusive relationship over time. I have great admiration for people who are able to do that. Fairly few of us can. Instead we have second marriages, third marriages; people keep trying, hoping that this time it will work; occasionally it does, when the partners have learned about living with another being and tele has entered the relationship.

DAG: So what we find in sociometry is that people are moving along in the path of life in different social atoms and happen not to share all these atoms with everybody. What we dream of in a marriage is to share all our social atoms with our life partner. But often, after having been attracted to each other originally, sexually and so on, the attraction between a husband and wife fades. Then the partners may begin to move around, find new social atoms and develop different roles with their new partners.

Why do you think people are so afraid of sociometry?

ZERKA: Because it creates a socioatomic revolution. Having a child or somebody dying in your life, just in the course of nature, is a revolution. Asking people to reveal their true preferences can create a revolution in existing relationships. Sociometry can also give a deathblow to an established relationship.

People in groups have a fear of being rejected. In our world being rejected is one of the worst things that can happen to us. Moreno would ask: 'Is it the rejection itself that you are worried about or is it the person who rejects you that you are concerned with? Who is rejecting you? Looking at this objectively, do you really want to be chosen by that person? Is it someone you want or are you simply reacting to the rejection? Rejection is so pejorative; it has a negative connotation in our culture. But think: What would have happened to Jesus Christ if he had not been rejected? He could not have lived his role.' He taught us to separate the rejection from the being of the rejecting person and, even if you were hurt by the person's rejection, to look at that hurt objectively; after all, not everyone has to love or want us. It depends on how important that person is to us. The rejection can also become a new way of looking at ourselves and at the way we build relationships.

Our fear of rejection is a hangover from our childhood and the rejections suffered there, which have not been healed. We need to heal them and become objective about our choices, whether they be mutual positive, mutual negative or incongruous, that is, positive versus negative. If you want someone and that person rejects you in turn on a specific criterion, that is painful; but on another criterion that person might choose you. Rejection is rarely total; there are objectionable people we reject, yet when we see their suffering in psychodrama, that rejection may well change, becoming either neutral or even positive.

As mentioned earlier, sociometry is directed towards daily life activities. Choices that we make in our daily lives are related to other human beings in the here-and-now. A sociogram makes these choices of attraction and rejection within a group visible. It shows the hierarchy of the group from the most chosen star to the sociometric isolates. The sociogram depicts the outcome of the choices based on a relevant criterion. For example, 'With whom would you like to do your homework?' would be a criterion suitable in the context of a school, as would 'With whom do you want to work on this scientific experiment?' The motive related to the first criterion could be 'X is good at arithmetic and might help me with mathematics', and for the second, 'We think differently about things and that stimulates our critical inquiry'. A pathological motive for either would here be, for example, 'I choose him because I am sexually attracted to him'. The sociogram reveals subjective feelings and thoughts, the motivation for choice points out hidden conflicts and disagreement that the group needs to work on to function better.

It is of interest here to refer to the German philosopher Hannah Arendt (1906–1975). She claims that all human activities take place within two spaces, the 'public' and the 'private'. The word 'public' means that everything that appears to the community is visible and audible to everyone, thus receiving the highest possible publicity and becoming reality. This is in opposition to the private world, where one is deprived of the reality created by being seen and heard, deprived of an objective relation to others. To the private world belong all activities that are not seen and heard by others such as dreams, thoughts, passions and fantasies.

We can experience the transformation between the private and the public when we try to tell a dream, a passion or a hope to somebody. Then the dream or passion is de-privatized or de-individualized; you do not keep it for yourself any longer. This means that the actions performed in a certain role will be seen and heard and judged by others. Some people might like these while others might resent the very same actions. However, somewhere between your own and the other perception the feeling of becoming real comes to life. As group psychotherapists we often deal with the difference between self-perception and the perception of others; how you express and understand yourself does not necessarily match what others see and hear. A person might have a certain intention with an action that is totally misunderstood or misinterpreted by others, which changes its impact. It is, therefore, not always possible to predict the outcome of an action.

According to Hannah Arendt the word 'public' also has another meaning, namely: the world itself, as it refers to what we have in common with others, which differs from what we refer to as 'privately owned'. Her concept of 'world' is the human creation (as opposed to earth or nature as a whole) as well as all affairs and concerns between humans that appear in the created world. To live together in this world means that a world of 'things' lies between its inhabitants, similar to a table *which is between those sitting around it. Everything that is 'between' in this world simultaneously connects and separates those who share it.*

Sociometric groups can only be formed in the public space. One can, however, question whether a family is a sociometric group or not, as sociometry usually implies the freedom to choose. As previously mentioned, a basic concept in the Morenian philosophy is the tele phenomenon. Tele, in the literal sense of the word, means 'distance'. But Moreno uses it as a term for something that creates and unites groups.

> *The innumerable varieties of attractions, repulsions and indifferences between individuals need a common denominator. A feeling is directed from one individual towards another. It has to be carried into distance. Just as we use the words teleperceptor, telephone, telencephalon, television, etc., to express action at a distance, so to express the simplest unit of* feeling transmitted from one individual to another *we use the term tele, τηλε, 'distant'.*
>
> *(J.L. Moreno 1953: 313–314, 1993: 158–159)*

Moreno made the tele factor responsible for the formation of groups and tele is definitely related to the role repertoire a person has in life. That means one person incorporates many roles, even roles that might contradict one another. We referred to this earlier when explaining the term 'autotele'. Roles are action-oriented and connect to roles in others. They are acted out in our daily lives and activities with these others. Hannah Arendt was also concerned with the actions of our daily lives. She was an action-oriented philosopher, as was Moreno.

Tele is directly related to sociometry. People gain a feeling of substance in the world by having their actions viewed and reflected by others. Tele is the human's compass to the world. Without it, we would be like the animals, directed by instincts.

ZERKA: In life we need to learn to stand aside and look at our relationships in the same way we learn to look at ourselves in the mirror, even though we may not always like what we see. When you are a child and are learning to brush your hair, that idiot in the mirror at first does not do it right. As you grow older and you see yourself in the mirror you ask: 'Is this the way I look to others? What do they see? What do I need to do to make myself beautiful or likeable or lovable?'

That's how we should be looking at our relationships. How do I come across to other people? If I want this relationship, if it is worth my investment in it, how do I accomplish that? What do I need to change in order to gain it? The 'Me Generation' does not seem to understand that. This egocentric 'Me-trend' all over the place is not very helpful for building human relations. I am not suggesting we should lose ourselves in a relationship, I am suggesting we grow in it.

DAG: For the child who sees itself in a mirror, the mirror does not change the character of the action, but reflects it from the opposite perspective. It combs its hair with the right hand, whereas the mirror image does the same with the left hand. It could be said that in a tele relationship, when one is mirrored in another person, that person sends back his/her reflection complete with his/her own human content.

ZERKA: As the child gets older it begins to wonder: 'Why do they like me? What do they see in me?' Or the reverse, too, of course. 'Why don't they like me? What do they see in me that makes me unlikeable to them?' If we are thinking people, we begin to look at that and question ourselves. I'm not talking about people who float through life like butterflies. I'm talking about most of us who have some real concerns about how we come across to the rest of the world. Because our families are not, in the main, satisfactorily nurturing, we are sensitive to this.

DAG: Do you remember a person whom you found absolutely lovable and adorable, while there were some people who said this is a horrible person?

ZERKA: Although it is a common experience for both boys and girls when they bring home a friend their parents do not like, I do not remember having had anything like that. I experienced the other. My parents brought me together with someone they thought would be wonderful for me to know and I found it to be painful. It was a little girl who was brought into my orbit. I was told she was so nice. What they did not know was that this child was having nightmares. We spent a couple of nights in the same bedroom, and she screamed all night long that she was seeing demons. This kid was a totally neurotic wreck. During the daytime she behaved very well so I now think she must have been completely suppressed by her parents. In those days good behaviour meant you were a good, quiet child and assumed to be happy as well. Today we know this is not necessarily true. All kinds of things go on behind that good behaviour, and it came out in this child's dreams at night.

I think it has to do with subjective perception. People have told me that I am intimidating. I do not find myself intimidating. My son told me when he was dating: 'Do you realize how intimidating you are to my girlfriends?'. I answered, 'No, I don't'. 'Well', he said, 'you are. You are powerful. You're intimidating to them.' I don't consider myself that powerful, but that is because I also know my own vulnerability, which perhaps some others cannot see or experience; they do not perceive it. It is useful to remember that even so-called strong persons have their Achilles heel.

DAG: Tell me about that. What happened to you in the moment he said that?

ZERKA: Well, I asked myself: 'What's wrong with me that I don't see that in me? If I don't see that in myself then other people may not see that in themselves either.' We don't know our own strength; we don't know how we affect other people. Obviously, the reverse is also true, we do not fully realize our weaknesses either. That's why we need role reversal.

DAG: Did you think your son was right?

ZERKA: Yes, I think that if his friends experience me that way, he is right. I mean, I do not think we told each other lies. The girls must have said that to him. It was then I realized that I had become powerful. There was a certain power in me even as a small child. My mother may have meant something like that when she once expressed to me: 'You are so different from my other children'. In principle that's nonsense. Every child is different. But what she was saying was (she was not as analytic as I am): 'I see something in you that is different from the others'. Possibly what she referred to is my strength. I remember when I was at a dance at school when I was 14 years old, waiting for my brothers, I made some remark about my brothers which only the Dutch would enjoy because it is a word game. In Dutch my word game was: *Waar zein mijn gebroeders?* The sentence should have been *Waar zein mijn broeders?* ('Where are my brothers?'). By adding *ge* in front of *broeders* I turned my brothers into a corporate entity. A senior class member, an older boy I did not know remarked: 'What an original child'. So I began to see that other people looked at me as original. What did that mean but being different? It is true that I felt a great deal different from my siblings, but I never asked any of them whether they felt different. It is not the kind of question one asked of one's relatives in those days. One asks that when one is mature and has that kind of connection: 'Did you ever feel different from all the others?' However, now I assume that, in fact, they did, because we led rather varied lives.

DAG: You are touching an interesting point in sociometry because some people feel a little exotically different. I can share that also.

ZERKA: You used the word 'exotic'. My husband pointed out to me that whenever we had groups coming to Beacon and he did sociometry with them I would pick the 'exotics' and I was not aware of that until he told me. But exotics often pick each other. They seem to mirror themselves with that.

DAG: So what we are saying is that you are seen differently by your students than by your son and his girlfriend, or your grandchildren; you are seen in various ways and that gives you a certain spectrum.

What I find interesting in sociometry is that groups come together and they are in essence goal-oriented, whatever that goal may be. Having a task or objective forces participants to choose with whom they want to interact, and lets them see who wants to interact with them. It is a profound experience to orient yourself in the here-and-now and in the world – with whom you can or cannot be a companion.

What I have experienced in psychodrama is that people feel 'I am not seen'. Could you say that to be seen by others, to be judged by others, to be viewed by others, creates the feeling of being real? Is that also valid for the psychotic person?

ZERKA: You don't even have to be psychotic. I have a number of students who say: 'I was never heard in my family'. This is where psychodrama of the family is so important. There used to be a saying: 'Little children should be seen but not heard', but, in fact, with that philosophy children are not seen properly either. It is important that children are heard and seen for who they are and not for what their parents want to see or want them to be. Here is a poem I wrote about that in *Love Songs to Life*. It is called 'The Right to Be Me'.

I am
not you
or he
or she.
I'm Me.

I am not short
or tall
or big
or small.
I'm Me.

I am not good
or bad
or gay
or sad.
I'm Me.

Oh, let me Be!

Don't you know?
Can't you see?
First of all
I'm Me!
(Z. Moreno 1971)

ZERKA: So we have to work on educating parents. First they have to clean up their own mess with their family of origin, to stop bringing that into their marriage, but also to be better prepared to see their children for who they truly are, unique beings. Kahlil Gibran spoke of this so movingly in *The Prophet*:

Your children are not your children.
They are the sons and daughters of Life's longing for itself.

They come through you but not from you,
And though they are with you yet they belong not to you.
(Gibran 1923)

My sense is that in the United States there is a genuine movement in the school system to help parents to see their children for the individuals they are and not for what they want to force them to be. Children need guidance along with love, nurturing and protection. Parents need to learn their role. Many of us have not had very satisfactory role models and we learn as we go along, sometimes in a hit-or-miss fashion. So much goes back to the family. If you are not seen and not heard in the family of origin, you go outside to be seen and heard. Why do you think young people form gangs? In the gang they become persons in interaction with other people, unfortunately often to the point of violence. Then parents ask: 'Why do you hang out with these bad boys?' Clearly because they are not rooted in their family.

DAG: They are not seen and not heard at home. In order to be seen and heard, Moreno created a sense of reality through psychodrama and sociometry.

ZERKA: That was his intention.

DAG: He also stated that the reason psychodrama as group psychotherapy could help psychotics is because when the patient acts out his or her delusions on the stage, the delusionary world becomes real.

ZERKA: Yes. Moreno not only accepted the delusionary world, he loved it and made it real.

DAG: Thus that world was seen and heard by others.

ZERKA: Absolutely, and respected for what it was.

DAG: Do you remember some of the sharing when a psychotic person worked on the stage?

ZERKA: The sharing was all done in action. When you shared as an auxiliary ego, you did not share in the way we do now because that already requires distance from the self on the part of the patient. The only sharing that went on was discussing with Moreno after the session what happened, how he had diagnosed and approached the patient, for what reasons, and how and whether he achieved what he meant to achieve, in other words, how he went about it, how he related to the patient and the effect of that interaction. We talked about what kind of progress the patient made but we did not do that with the patient present. That would have broken the surplus reality. He did not allow the objective reality to enter into the process until the patient, he felt, was strong enough to accept it. What was the patient's reality was for us *surplus* reality. Moreno played with that.

We had a patient who presented himself as the saviour, his kind of Jesus Christ. He stands naked on top of the hill and speaks the Sermon on the Mount; nobody is there, but for him a crowd is present. Next door, it just so happens, we have a novitiate where young novices come to test themselves and reflect before becoming nuns. The Mother Superior calls my husband and tells him there is a young man in the nude standing on the hill in our grounds. 'Could you please have him put some clothes on? We have these young women here, 17, 18 years old.' 'Sure', he told her, 'why not. I'll see what I can do.' He goes outside and up the hill. I accompany him. As he approaches the patient he says: 'You know, Jesus, it's wonderful what you are doing. We love to hear your speech. But it's a bit cool outside today. Would you mind going inside and putting your underpants on?' The patient obeys him without any trouble and does as he is requested. He had not been disrespected, the role was real: here he could be Jesus. If the patient would have questioned him, for instance, and asked him why he should, Moreno might have answered: 'None of your paintings show you in the nude'. Weave the reality into the other world of psychodrama where it can be useful. Speaking from the other perspective I asked Moreno: 'Did you tell the lady Abbess who he is?' He said: 'I did not think she would appreciate it'. But you see what I mean? He maintained the context within which this patient was operating and did not destroy it. He did not say to the patient: 'We know who you are and this is ridiculous'. He would not do that. He did not tell him: 'This woman next door wants you to get dressed because there are young women there'.

DAG: But he did subtly weave in that aspect too.

ZERKA: Yes, the fact that there is a reality out there as well: 'It's cool today'.

DAG: That is really beautiful. I think sociometry has been neglected because people are fearful that their own reality will be discarded. When we recall our childhood memories we sense that there was inner motivation for a choice, speaking in sociometric terms. That inner motivation is not respected. In the imaginary world we sometimes choose or reject someone because that person reminds us of our mother, for example, or 'I don't like very big men or women', because we relate that to our past world, it is not related to the here-and-now.

ZERKA: Correct. In other forms of psychotherapy therapists point this out to the client. That type of insight is not as helpful as correcting the past by repairing it first, as, for instance, through psychodrama. That makes it easier for the protagonist to discard the old neglect rather than carrying it into the present.

As I said before: *affirmation comes before negation.* We cannot give up what we have not had. If you are never seen or heard you can become schizophrenic or at least disturbed. You talk with yourself because you are the only one who hears you, who listens to you, who experiences you; or you make your imaginary companions. You may be right about the technique of going back into childhood in psychotherapy and psychodrama; I do not believe that every psychodrama has to go back into the past. But when I hear a person saying: 'My wife never listens to me; that is exactly what happened to me in my family and I get enraged', then we go back into that family of origin. We can repair the past and the protagonist can give it up so that at least he does not get enraged any more and can deal with the present adequately.

One characteristic of human beings is that their actions are similar and different at the same time. We reveal who we are through our actions. What we are refers to characteristics and gifts of personality. One can be, for example, a gifted singer or painter without ever having been on the stage or sold one single painting. One can be a very talented person but that does not mean one has ever actualized that role. Moreno says that spontaneity is the arm and hand of creativity. Who we are will always be how others see us, whereas what we are remains private. Particularly in the Jungian form emphasis is on 'what we are' instead of 'who we are'. In Jung's psychology 'Persona' is the mask we wear towards the world, e.g. the doctor, the lawyer. There is very little uniqueness or individuality in the Persona. The individual can hide behind this mask.

Jungian work is mostly done through the analysis of dreams or through working with the unconscious or the Shadow. Moreno looks differently at the distinction between the conscious and the unconscious. For him action carries truth in itself in the encounter with other people.

> *Thus the distinction between conscious and unconscious has no place in a psychology of the creative act. It is* logificatio post festum. *We make use of it as a popular fiction only to map out a science of characters of the impromptu act.*
>
> *(J.L. Moreno 1973: 42)*

Our actions really show our uniqueness. So to what extent can we hide behind our Persona? Instead we show who we are through our visible behaviour. We are rejected or affirmed through our interaction with others.

For example, a young boy who behaves badly in school by carrying weapons threatens the security, disturbs the class, and is designated 'the bad boy'. This is how he is seen by others and how he learns to play the role. His problematic past with abuse and neglect certainly can make us understand his behaviour. Still his past can only be heard, it can't be seen or experienced by the group in his daily life out there. Only in psychodrama can we make it visible and heard. Group psychotherapy both emphasizes and highlights our actions. In this process change can take place. In other words, we can only change in interaction with other people, in the here-and-now.

ZERKA: What is largely misunderstood about sociometry is that enabling people to make their own choices is evidence of our respect for them. We are not judgemental, we make a judgement. There is a difference.

DAG: Is judgement involved when we make a choice or when a person says: 'I only want to be me'?

ZERKA: Yes, on both counts. At the same time, if you ask a person: 'Who is this me?' they do not know, except when we begin to explore it in terms of: 'Let's see your role structure. Let's see your social atom; then we get some sense of who you are and you can see yourself. Let's find out how other people relate to this being in this role structure and in that social atom.' Yes, there is no question that judgement is necessary but if I say to you: 'I just want to be me', you could ask me: 'What does that mean? What is that? Who do you think you are? Show me.'

DAG: Clients of mine would be extremely offended if I asked that.

ZERKA: I say: 'Tell me who you are, tell me what you mean to yourself. Then I can judge whether I have the same perception of you.' I have difficulty with people who come to me; sometimes they are people I hardly know, and they ask me questions I can't answer. I remember a student of Moreno's who had just been married two days before; he came to introduce his wife to us. They stayed overnight in our house and that was our only contact with this young woman. The next morning he came to ask me: 'What do you think of my wife?' I refused to answer him in a direct way. 'I have barely met her; we just had an exchange of a few polite words with each other, so the question is not fair. But I want to ask you: What do *you* think of her? You're the one who chose her. On what basis did you make that decision? I, on the contrary, have not met her before, so this is an unrealistic question. I did not make that choice, you did. You think you know her, you picked her, you tell me what you think of your wife.'

The obvious reason he asked me is that he thought he had made a mistake and, in fact, the marriage ended not long afterwards. 'What do you think of my wife or husband?' does not make sense and yet some people enter marriage in that way. It's all very well to have a spontaneous 'clicking' with another person, but then there comes a time when a couple should say: 'Now we need to explore the relationship beyond this clicking that we have, to see what we have mutually satisfactory in common'. There the role structure comes in.

DAG: What do you think is the difference between the sociometric group and the family?

ZERKA: Choice. In the family the couple themselves chose to be together in the beginning, although the choice may be based on false premises and may wear thin over the years. Children will say to their parents when they are being punished, 'I did not choose to be born', which, by the way, from the spiritual point of view is not true. I think they did choose to be born to these parents but they find the going too hard. So they will say: 'I did not choose to be born. You chose to have me.' At least it is a choice in this earthly life, a choice for our soul or spirit. From the sociometric point of view, we know that unrequited loves, non-mutual choices, are the most painful. For a child who finds itself not loved the way it deserves, certainly its birth feels like a non-choice. The family is or at least was first a biological grouping.

The sociometric grouping is of a different order of choice. In a family authority rests in the parents and in a given structure related to sex, age, culture and procreation. In sociometric groups these factors do not apply in the same way. The sociometric group is an intentional community. For instance, a sociometric group is always in a state of change. After the purpose of coming together around its criterion is fulfilled by all its members, the group may dissolve and a new criterion has to be born. The family is far more static. In sociometry, leadership is chosen of the group, by the group and for the group. That is not the case in the family and, in fact, there is often a good deal of rebellion.

DAG: Group psychotherapy has lately taught me something new: when not to say things.

ZERKA: You mean when to speak and when to be totally silent. It is interesting that you speak of that because I have a similar awareness, for instance with people who have had or are having extramarital affairs. My sense is that they should especially not talk about them with their partners or with their friends. Many of them are weighed down by feelings of guilt: 'Oh God, I have to tell my husband, I have to tell my wife.' Don't. When they come to me and ask me what they should do, I question them: 'Is the outside relationship still relevant?' Many times the answer is: 'No'. 'How recent is it?' 'Oh, it happened two years ago.' 'Are you still in touch?' 'No.' 'Are you telling me it is completely over, except for the guilt you carry about it?' 'Yes.' Then I ask: 'What are you trying to do? You have lived with your mate so many years, do you intend to separate?' 'No.' 'You have not spoken about it?' 'No, I couldn't.' 'So how can it possibly help except that you can release your guilt about it. Are you trying to punish your mate? Is s/he guilty of the same thing? Are you angry with her/him for something you have been made to suffer? If so, let's work on it, but if that is not the case, you may do far more harm than good.'

Let me give you a specific case. Remember the attitude of many in the 60s and 70s ?: 'You must be up front with everybody, *let it all hang out*, be totally honest, and don't hide anything.' I will never forget a relationship revealed to us in the group by a student from Canada. He felt very guilty; he had just a month ago completed an extramarital affair. He met this woman while his wife was lecturing somewhere; he had accompanied her and they both met this other lady. She was a representative from the university where his wife was speaking and had found them a place to stay, and was their guide for that period. He became involved with her. Officially he went on business but actually he went to meet her. They had this relationship for a while and mutually decided to end it. When it is not mutually ended, the other party will suffer and hound the former partner, and that feels terrible.

The protagonist's question was whether he should tell his wife. All the young people in the group were asked for their opinion and one and all, without exception, said: 'Oh yes, you must tell her. After all, it is over now and you must be up-front with her.' I happened to know the wife as she was my student. He was not, but she had interested him in psychodrama and he came alone to work on this situation. I knew that his wife adored him; he was the love of her life. I asked him the same questions mentioned above: 'Is it over?' 'Yes.' 'Are you sure?' 'Yes, it is really over and done with.' 'Does your wife know or suspect anything?' 'No.' In fact, the other lady left Canada, returned to her own country, and they arranged not to be in further contact, by mail or any other way. So I say to him: 'Don't say or breathe a word'. He followed that recommendation because I also added: 'You would break her heart. Is that your intention?' He shook his head, negatively. That is not yet the end of the story. Five years or so later his wife developed a serious heart condition, which eventually contributed to her death. He becomes the most wonderful companion, takes care of her to the end, in a loving way. Was he still expiating his guilt? Maybe, and there may have been other reasons behind that, but the fact is that they lived harmoniously, at least as she experienced their life; she called and told me after her first attack how wonderfully devoted he was to her. I thought to myself, this woman would have died of a heart condition five years ago if he had told her, and how would he have felt then and what would have become of their relationship? Now she has a good companion who takes care of her and loves her, and the children are not hurt either. He was magnificent. The danger of total openness in a marriage can be great; we do not know the possible consequences.

DAG: I think it is equally valid for the training group and the therapy group that people also have to learn what can be revealed about themselves. I had a woman in a group, a therapist, who was a prostitute in the past and at an international meeting in the professional world she opened up about that in a session.

ZERKA: To what purpose?

DAG: I guess she wanted to be honest about it, and she thought it was okay.

ZERKA: It did not turn out to be okay.

DAG: No. Later she had terrible problems about it and was exposed to slander. She learned that she should be aware *where, how, and to whom* to reveal this part of her past. It is not the focus of this book, but feeling shame about yourself and wanting to be yourself is really standing on the edge between the private and the public space, because your shame should remain private.

ZERKA: It is a very delicate question, a question of adequacy, which does not mean adjustment, but being in tune with. You mirror yourself through other human beings and through figures in your inner world and you must be able to move around in that ambivalence. So in adequacy there is also judgement. Moreno expressed his concept of spontaneity as 'an adequate response to a new situation or a new response to an old situation'. One may be tempted to assume that the word 'adequate' is meant as a way of adapting to a situation by taking into account social norms. That was not Moreno's intention because then spontaneity and opportunism would be the same. For Moreno a spontaneous person is a disciplined person, but the discipline comes from within and is not imposed from without.

The word adequate comes from the Latin word ad-aeque *which means 'to make similar, to equate'.* Ad *is a preposition controlling the following accusative and means 'against, in the direction of', i.e., it contains a movement, a direction.* Aeques *means 'similar', similar condition, similar in size. Movement and balance thus are expressed by the word 'adequate'. It is not a static expression, a passive response, but contains the ability to think and to act reasonably with regard to the situation by taking into account one's own point of view as well as that of the surroundings. The person has the ability to act from a kind of transcendent point. A precondition for this ability is that a person acts spontaneously. Moreno said that the word* sponte *means 'from within the self'. Thus, it is neither right nor wrong. The word* sponte *also means 'with the consent of someone else' or 'with the good recollection of someone else', which refers to a kind of awareness or attention and includes another. At the same time it means to be one's own person, to express one's freedom. This leads to the idea that a person has the freedom to act, but that is not identical to free will.*

DAG: As we said before, when you work with sociometry the criterion has to be valid within the context in which you are working. If you work with the staff in a psychiatric hospital, for instance, relevant criteria would be: 'With whom would you like to work the night shift? With whom would you like to distribute medication?' An irrelevant criterion would be: 'With whom would you like to go on holiday?' or 'Whom would you want to date?' Those criteria are outside of the context of the group.

ZERKA: Yes, because they are external to the setting. In the hospital you have to deal with those interactions, the others are external. It creates problems if you work on irrelevant criteria. The boundaries are crossed. One of the things Moreno taught is that we must choose a criterion which can be carried out in reality for the entire group. Because with whom you go on vacation is not within the group, it pulls people away from the group. Besides, it should be a criterion which the sociometrist has the authority to carry out. Obviously, you do not have authority in the external situations. Working with irrelevant criteria is what Moreno called 'near-sociometry'. Sociometry is reality- and action-based and therefore the criteria have to be the same and the action should be of the kind that can be actually carried out. It has to be kept clean, otherwise it becomes impure and the results utterly useless or even harmful.

DAG: That is where I see a lot of damage done.

ZERKA: It is anti-democratic and a lesson for people to learn. Sociometry is democracy exercised in action. There are different hierarchies for different groupings and they are fluid. 'You cannot step twice into the same river.' It is a democracy by full participation, not merely by representation. It is not understood enough that Moreno never wrote that sociometry involves likes and dislikes. These watered-down versions that researchers describe as sociometric are based on a false premise.

Moreno never asked: 'Who do you like?' or 'Who do you not like?' He never used those words at all. He questioned: 'With whom do you like to work?' or 'With whom do you like to study?' or 'With whom do you like to share a room?' Non-sociometric studies do not connect the 'like' with the verbs 'to do this or that with' because these researchers are not action people; they are observers, not doers. Sociometry and role interactions are tightly linked; without a verb, verbs being action words, the research is invalid as sociometric and should not be so designated. It does not carry the essential action link, that of the role interaction. But if I ask you: 'With whom do you want to work in this setting?' and see if that person chooses you as well, and if I have the authority to reorganize the group based on the choices made, this is not an investigation, this is an action test; it has to lead to action, to satisfaction in life itself. To the extent it does not do that it is not sociometry. It is a test for the people in the group to cooperate with each other and the sociometrist, to be their own researchers. They are the ones who need it. I, the investigator do not need it for my ego. I'm doing this to make a more cohesive group. Maybe the words 'research' and 'investigator' are misleading. Perhaps we should call the process 'cohesion and action building'. Sociometry makes the group members co-researchers, not objects for an outsider to investigate. Besides, what reason would you as research object have to tell me the truth about yourself if you did not get some satisfaction out of it? One of the outcomes of sociometry is that the people involved obtain an 'optimum of satisfaction possible' from the procedure.

Chapter 17

The Tragic Self

Surplus reality versus the world in which we appear

In his book The Theatre of Spontaneity *Moreno emphasized the creative act and that roles played in life and those on the psychodrama stage have a merely superficial similarity. In fact, they have an entirely different meaning. He writes:*

> *In life our sufferings are real, our hunger, our anger are real. It is the difference between reality and fiction; or, as Buddha said: 'What is terrible to be, is lovely to see.' [One characteristic] of the creative act is that it means acting* sui generis. *During the process of living we are far more acted upon than acting. It is the difference between a creature and a creator.*
>
> *(J.L. Moreno 1973: 43)*

What we call reality is created on stage in the action which takes place between the people involved – a reality that relates to our Tragic Self. The Tragic Self has been explored by Dr Ruth Padel in her books, In and Out of the Mind: The Greek Image of the Tragic Self *and* Whom Gods Destroy. *The Tragic Self should be understood as the artistic need to voice the pain of life and death. The pain of our passage through life involves experiences like punishment, disease, war, or loss, to name only a few.*

Humans experience emotions but in the Greek drama they are not a subjective possession of man – they belong to the gods. Through the gods of Aries, Aphrodite, Hera we experience, for example, passion, eroticism, beauty and jealousy. We say someone 'has been hit by Cupid's arrow', meaning they have fallen in love. But the gods also send madness to these people, and sometimes they want to destroy them. The Furies drive those who break the taboos of life into madness by rage, revenge and envy; their goal is final destruction.

Another form of madness, the Dionysian 'frenzy', can lead to ecstasy or hubris, in which humans lose their human form, are disgraced, shameful. All of these emotions and contradictions are experienced by the Tragic Self. It derails us from the daily tracks of life. It brings melancholia, sadness and hallucinations. The Tragic Self, which takes us out of the world of god-induced emotions as portrayed in ancient Greek drama, is experienced and created in situ *by a group through the psychodrama, the soul in action.*

The Tragic Self relates to a soul's history, which is quite different from the ego's history. Important moments in the ego's history are marriage, birth, graduations, diseases, or divorce, for example. The soul's history contains elements that seem to be unrelated. It is one of images, such as a movie, a meeting, a face, or shame, for example. When we ask for the soul's history we can also ask, 'How many times have you died in your life?' Therefore, the soul's truth does not necessarily have anything in common with truth of the ego. In the act of suicide we can see the difference between the soul's history and case history, or the history of the ego.

When someone commits suicide we often ask ourselves, 'Why did he kill himself? He had everything and seemed to be happy.' We try to find visible outer circumstances to make it understandable, but we will always come back to the initial question, 'Why did he do it?' The Tragic Self speaks in dark images, in images of madness and self-destruction. In suicide we see the Tragic Self propelled from within the individual and acted out in the external world. Another aspect of the Tragic Self is brought to light in the case of assassination. There the Tragic Self is embodied by the assassin or murderer. The connection between tragedy and the Tragic Self is destruction and violent death.

On the psychodrama stage these different realities are fused together in a massa confusa *which became for Moreno surplus reality. This reality is artistic and creative; in it we experience the frenzy within the creative act rather than in its end. Every moment is a birth. The Tragic Self manifests in action on the psychodrama stage, where the protagonist's soul leads the action and the director guides the protagonist to expand and intensify this dramatic tension of life, his or her inner dialogues, falling apart, doubts, and different moods. Very often, after such sessions protagonists are shocked by how they described their mothers, fathers, or children. If our parents were to see one of our psychodramas dealing with them, they might say we are liars, because in the psychodrama we act out what happened and what never happened. Stanislavski said in* An Actor Prepares*: 'In talking about a genius*[1] *you would not say that he lies; he sees reality with different eyes from ours' (Stanislavski 1936: 53).*

It is the Tragic Self that is shared with the group in action. The catharsis is not merely a way of immediately finding a solution, such as 'What do we do now?' The therapeutic effect of surplus reality is the healing experience of the Tragic Self having been seen and heard by others as well as dealt with by oneself. Psychodrama has successfully worked with very ill people with hallucinations and delusions because, in the true sense of the word, Moreno gave substance to their hallucinatory or surreal world. He let the protagonist wander around in it; he let the protagonist explore his/her delusions.

As Mary Watkins writes, the word 'hallucination' derives from the Latin word (h)allucinari *and means 'to wander in mind; to talk idly' (Watkins 1986). One of the most characteristic images of madness is that of the wanderer who goes alone and away. The lone wanderer is a central theme in many Greek tragedies. Through the psychodramatic exploration the hallucinatory and imaginal world, so private before, kept in such a shadow existence which was not understood, is brought out on the stage and acted upon; it is experienced as if it were real.*

When Moreno treated Karl, as described in Psychodrama: Second Volume *in 'The Psychodrama of Adolf Hitler', neither Goering was there nor Hitler. All these persons were played by others 'as if' and, thereby, created a tragic tension and reality. Zerka and J.L. Moreno pointed out that psychodrama provided the psychotic person with an audience. In all my years of directing psychodrama, I have seen that every human being is capable of distinguishing between the psychodramatic reality as it relates to the Tragic Self and the Daily Life Self. This means that one can distinguish between the reality of life and that of the psychodrama stage. Nevertheless, time and again we see how the magic 'as if' takes over during the psychodramatic enactment and becomes 'as'. In that sense, surplus reality and the world outside are in contradiction as well as in agreement; fantasy and reality can destroy as well as complement one another. How can we define the world outside in which we live, the world where we work and exist, where we have to act and interact with other human beings?*

Hannah Arendt writes:

> *The world men are born into contains many things, natural and artificial, living and dead, transient and sempiternal, all of which have in common that they* appear *and hence are meant to be seen, heard, touched, tasted and smelled, to be perceived by sentient creatures endowed with the appropriate sense organs . . .*

> *In this world which we enter, appearing from a nowhere, and from which we disappear into a nowhere* Being and Appearing coincide.
>
> *(Arendt 1978: 19)*

For Hannah Arendt, appearance, as perceived through the five senses, is the equivalent of being and of feeling real. We are as we appear and vice versa. There is no need for proof of existence or depth of meaning beyond simple appearance.

What is unique to psychodrama is that it is dramatic acting with other people and, therefore, one 'appears' and is seen and heard by oneself as well as by others. One is in interaction, one is related and one feels related. Psychodrama has the capacity to add meaning to something that might originally have been boring, painful or seemingly worthless. In this process the protagonist experiences the freedom of action. Action as a beginning is rooted in natality since it is the actualization of freedom; it carries with it the capacity to perform miracles, that is, to introduce what is totally unexpected. Arendt claims:

> *It is in the nature of beginning that something new is started which cannot be expected from whatever may have happened before. This character of startling unexpectedness is inherent in all beginnings . . . The fact that man is capable of action means that the unexpected can be expected from him, that he is able to perform what is infinitely improbable. And this again is possible only because each man is unique, so that with each birth something uniquely new comes into the world.*
>
> *(Arendt 1958: 177–178)*

To act means, therefore, to be able to take the initiative and to do the unanticipated, to exercise that capacity for freedom which was given to us the moment we came into the world. To act and to be free are, in this respect, synonymous: to be free means to engage in action, while through action our capacity for freedom is actualized.

> *Moreno describes spontaneity as a form of energy which is non-conservable and which must be spent as it emerges. Its outcome is unpredictable and when linked to creativity it is most valuable, producing something not pre-existing, something that was not there before and at times totally unrelated to earlier events.*
>
> *(Z. Moreno 1998)*

Thus, both Moreno and Hannah Arendt were clearly oriented towards action. Through spontaneity we feel free to master new situations and surprises in life; to encounter old situations with new reactions as a result is, therefore, appropriate because nothing can ever be as it was before. Inspiration is the first agent to add to The Water of Life. The psychodrama activates inspiration in the protagonist and in the group members. So often nowadays we are passive consumers of television, work, theatre and other diversions. However, in psychodrama we turn into actors and creators. In psychotherapy many people complain that they 'are not seen or heard'. They feel bored. The Water of Life has disappeared. Psychodrama brings this water back because it can turn 'normal' life into a tragedy, a comedy or a satire.

With the sociometric approach, Moreno dealt with the world as it appears. A goal of sociometry is that of orienting a person in the world in which s/he lives and appears. Group psychotherapy is meant to make him/her aware of how s/he is experienced by other people. The group, like the ancient Greek chorus in a drama, will voice and judge actions as well as share. In the sharing phase that ends every psychodrama, participants share their experiences on the stage as well as from their life outside. It can also be sharing from the Tragic Self. The Tragic Self is experienced only in the theatre and in the drama. When Moreno created psychodrama he moved the audience onto the stage and made everybody a participant in the creative act.

Healing through surplus reality, therefore, includes the experience of emotions from the Tragic Self as well as an orientation in the world in which the person lives.

Epilogue

Zerka T. Moreno

In reviewing what has been produced here it became clear to me that my thinking has expanded over the years into realms which I never discussed with Moreno but which now seem to me to be both part of my own development in this field as well as building on Moreno's oeuvre. Any field that needs to survive in the world of thought must continue to grow and develop. However, there is in this book a blueprint which we owe to Moreno. I am specifically thinking of a postulate stated in his paper 'Sociometry and the Cultural Order' (J.L. Moreno 1943). It is a basic building block of his ideas. Moreno questioned the correctness of interpreting the Greek notion that the psyche is located inside the body. In fact, the Greeks divided the soul into the body soul and the free soul. The free soul was not anchored in the body. In medieval times Giordano Bruno (Dominican monk, pantheist, 1548–1600) was burned at the stake as a heretic for declaring similar ideas.

In the aforementioned paper Moreno stated that it is conceivable that the psyche is not located in the body but that instead the body is enveloped by the psyche. Assuming this inside–outside of psychic matter is correct it makes it easier to understand why we can contact other persons' ideas, thoughts, images and even facts about their lives consciously unknown to us.

In a group of psychodramatists consisting of forty-five participants a young woman protagonist needed to work on the sudden death of her father. He died in his sleep in bed lying next to his wife, her mother. This sudden event made it impossible for her to complete her farewell to him and she proceeded to do this in her psychodrama. She chose for her father a young man whom she knew because they worked in the same mental health clinic. It became clear during the sharing that they had never discussed this traumatic event in her life. So imagine the amazement of the protagonist as well as the rest of the group when the auxiliary ego told her that his own father had died in the very same way.

This phenomenon occurs very frequently in psychodrama, namely that an unknown event in the chosen auxiliary ego's life is brought to light specifically in the sharing. We are now beginning to accept this mysterious effect because we assume it is related to the tele phenomenon. Tele operates in mysterious ways but it becomes less mysterious if we assume that it is clearly linked to the psyche outside the body phenomenon. In fact, just as Moreno described in *Who Shall Survive?*, the finding that some of the inmates and housemothers at the school in Hudson had what he called a large 'acquaintance volume' whereas others had a much smaller acquaintance range, it occurs to me that this is again another aspect of the psyche outside the body being related to the dimension of tele (J.L. Moreno 1993: 131). It is not merely an effect of cognition.

I hope it is clear that, while we have ranged over a large area in this book, we have never lost sight of Moreno's construction of his system as standing under the umbrella of sociometry within which psychodrama and group psychotherapy are contained. Moreno began with group psychotherapy in Vienna with the prostitutes, one person as the therapeutic support of the other. The idea of therapeutic support was later developed into sociometry, with which he planned a scientific–artistic revolution of society. In this he joined Freud who called himself a 'scientific artist'. Unfortunately Freud never moved into the group dimension.

When Moreno discovered that what really motivates human beings to live fully is spontaneity and creativity he began to look for a model, which he found in the drama, as an example of how people 'go astray' in life. Moreno had already experimented with improvisational drama with the children in the gardens of Vienna in the first decade of the century. This inspired him to create the Theatre of Spontaneity which was a rebellion against the so-called legitimate drama. Out of the Theatre of Spontaneity the Therapeutic Theatre, a theatre of healing, later called psychodrama, emerged. It should be clearly understood that Moreno considered his sociometric system to be a revolutionary category. Therefore, when people come to psychodrama in no matter what role, professional, patient or student, they want a revolution in their lives. The threefold system of psychodrama, sociometry and group psychotherapy has not been fully accepted by the establishment, itself a cultural conserve. Because of their strength, based on spontaneity and creativity, perhaps they never will be.

Notes

Introduction

1 'From the instant where for the first navigators a new land came into view, to that at which they set foot on the coast, to the instant in which such savant can convince himself that he came to be a witness to a hitherto to him unknown phenomenon, to that one where he commenced to measure the weight of his observation.' (Translation by the authors)

Chapter 1

1 The word 'cosmos' is a Greek word and its meaning is: universe, system, or order of the world (*Weltordnung*), the whole of mankind. It is, therefore, a word that encompasses man and his entire surroundings, micro- and macrocosm.

Chapter 2

1 'It is the surprise created by a new image or a new association of images that one must regard as the most important element of progress in physical sciences, because it is the amazement which stimulates the unimaginative and cold logic and sets it in motion to establish new coordinates.' (Translation by the authors)
2 J.L. Moreno regarded empathy as a one-way process. He believed there is a process taking place in both persons which goes beyond a mutual empathy. He called this process, in which thoughts and feelings of both participants interweave, 'two-way empathy'. Both enter each other's minds and influence one another. This phenomenon J.L. Moreno called 'tele'.
3 Rationale: statement of reasons, fundamental reason, logical basis

Chapter 6

1 Eastern religions put an emphasis on existential experiences. The purpose of its exercises is to liberate man from a view of the world which disguises the

world's truth. One of the major religions of this kind is Zen. Its path leads to the awakening of our divine essence and its proof in the mature acceptance and mastering of the world. Zen is different from other forms of Buddhism in its independence from concepts and images, the inexorability of its demands, the directness of its practical exercises and the imperturbability with which it aims at the core of our essence that is unconditional and not affected by suffering. Zen teaches us to be in touch with this core of our essence under all circumstance and conditions – serene, faithful, true, free and independent.

Chapter 7

1 The Dadaists capitalized on the element of chance, and the works they created provide challenges for the mind as well as for the eye. They highlighted the importance of the creative act over the finished work, and their professional goal was the negation, or at least the redirection, of all art – visual and literary. Their work reflected a new role: allowing the irrational. However, the negative side was the total nihilism of the Dada posture (Rubin 1990).
2 Beacon: signal, signal fire on pole or hills, lighthouse, guide or warning. Beacon, NY, was also the place where Moreno lived and worked.
3 'The cosmic experience of religion is the strongest and most noble reason for research in the natural sciences. The deepest and most gripping feeling of which we are capable is the experience of the mystic. From that alone true science arises.' (Translation by the authors)

Chapter 8

1 'Whenever a living creature is gravely ill, every turn for the better involves an element of mystery, even when the physician has recognized and eliminated the cause of sickness. For the physician cannot act alone; side by side with his outside intervention something inside the patient must lend a helping hand if a cure is to be accomplished. At the crucial moment something is at work that might best be compared to the flow of a spring.' (Translation by the authors)
2 Lourdes is a village in southern France (Dép. Hautes-Pyrénées) where in a nearby grotto the Virgin Mary is said to have appeared in 1858. Because of its miraculous springs it has become a place of pilgrimage with many reported miracle cures.

Chapter 12

1 Dirndl dresses are designed like traditional costumes which can be found in Bavaria and Austria.

Chapter 17

1 Genius: an exceptional, natural capacity of intellect, especially as shown in creative and original work in music, etc.

Bibliography

Arendt, H. (1958) *The Human Condition*, Chicago: University of Chicago Press.

—— (1969) *On Violence*, San Diego: Harcourt Brace & Co.

—— (1978) *The Life of the Mind*, San Diego: Harcourt Brace & Co.

Augustinus, A. (1955) *Bekenntnisse*, Paderborn: Schöningh.

Blomkvist, L.D. and Rützel, T. (1994) 'Surplus Reality and Beyond', in P. Holmes, M. Karp and M. Watson (eds) *Psychodrama since Moreno: Innovations in Theory and Practice*, London: Routledge.

Boorstin, D.J. (1993) *The Creators: A History of Heroes of the Imagination*, New York: Vintage Books.

Bremmer, J. (1983) *The Early Greek Concept of the Soul*, Princeton, NJ : Princeton University Press.

Breton, A. (1937) *L'amour Fou*, Paris: Le Club Français du Livre.

—— (1949) *Nadja*, Paris: Gallimard.

—— (1965) in M. Nadeau (ed.) *The History of Surrealism*, New York: The Macmillan Company.

—— (1972) *Manifestoes of Surrealism*, Ann Arbor: The University of Michigan Press.

Conty, P. (1992) 'The Geometry of the Labyrinth', *Parabola* Summer: 14.

Eckhart, M. (1963) 'Reden der Unterweisung', in J. Quint (ed.) *Ins Neuhochdeutsche übertragen*, Frankfurt: Insel-Verlag.

Einstein, A. (1984) in C. Einiger and C. Waldemar (eds) *Die schönsten Gebete der Welt*, Munich: Südwest-Verlag.

Florman, S. (1997) 'The Humane Engineer', *Technology Review* 100, 5: 59.

Franz, M.-L. von (1992) *Psyche and Matter*, Boston: Shambhala.

Gibran, K. (1923) *The Prophet*, New York: Alfred A. Knopf

Kerényi, K. (1948) *Der göttliche Arzt–Studien über Asklepios und seine Kultstätte*, Basel: Ciba AG.

Meier, C.A. (1989) *Healing Dream and Ritual*, Einsiedeln: Daimon Verlag.

Moreno, J.L. (1943) 'Sociometry and the Cultural Order', *Sociometry: A Journal of Interpersonal Relations*, 3: 3.

—— (ed.) (1945) *Group Psychotherapy: A Symposium*, Beacon, NY: Beacon House Inc.
—— (1953) *Who Shall Survive?: Foundations of Sociometry, Group Psychotherapy and Sociodrama*, Beacon, NY: Beacon House, Inc.
—— (1965) 'Therapeutic Vehicles and the Concept of Surplus Reality', *Group Psychotherapy* 18: 211-216.
—— (1973) *The Theatre of Spontaneity*, Beacon, NY: Beacon House, Inc.
—— (1977) *Psychodrama: First Volume*, Beacon, NY: Beacon House, Inc.
—— (1987) from *Group Psychotherapy, Psychodrama and Sociometry* 4: 273–303 as quoted in J. Fox (ed.) *The Essential Moreno: Writings on Psychodrama, Group Method, and Spontaneity*, New York: Springer.
—— (1993) *Who Shall Survive?: Foundations of Sociometry, Group Psychotherapy and Sociodrama* (Student Edition), McLean, VA: American Society of Group Psychotherapy and Psychodrama.
Moreno, J.L. and Moreno, Z.T. (1975a) *Psychodrama: Second Volume*, Beacon, NY: Beacon House, Inc.
—— (1975b) *Psychodrama: Third Volume*, Beacon, NY: Beacon House, Inc.
Moreno, Z. (1971) *Love Songs to Life*, Beacon, NY: Beacon House Inc.
—— (1993) *Love Songs to Life*, (2nd ed.) Princeton, NJ: American Society of Group Psychotherapy and Psychodrama.
—— (1998) 'The Many Faces of Drama', *Dramascope* 14, 1.
Otto, W.F. (1981) *Dionysus: Myth and Cults*, Woodstock, CT: Spring Publishers.
Padel, R. (1995) *Whom Gods Destroy: Elements of Greek and Tragic Madness*, Princeton, NJ: Princeton University Press.
Plaut, F. (1986) *A Critical Dictionary of Jungian Analysis*, London: Routledge.
Rubin, W.S. (1990) *Dada, Surrealism, and their Heritage*, New York: Harry N. Abrams.
Simon, E. (1982) *The Ancient Theatre*, London: Methuen.
Sjölin, J. (1981) *Den Surrealistiska Erfarenheten*, Aarhus: Kalejdoskop Verlag.
Stanislavski, K. (1948) *My Life in Art*, New York: Theater Arts Books.
Watkins, M. (1986) *Invisible Guests: The Development of Imaginal Dialogues*, Woodstock, CT: Spring Publications, Inc.
Winkler, J. and Zeitlin, F. (1990) *Nothing to Do with Dionysos: Athenian Drama in its Social Context*, Princeton, NJ: Princeton University Press.

Index

For Product Safety Concerns and Information please contact our EU representative GPSR@taylorandfrancis.com Taylor & Francis Verlag GmbH, Kaufingerstraße 24, 80331 München, Germany